Mel Bay Presents

Basic C6th Nonpedal Lap Steel Method

By DeWitt Scott

CD CONTENTS

1 Tuning [:24]	20 Joy To The World [:52]
2 Sidewalks of Nashville [:49]	21 On Top Of Old Smokey [:40]
3 Sandy Ann [:42]	22 Sweet Hour of Prayer [1:22]
4 Banks of the Ohio [:59]	23 Country Style Steel [1:06]
5 Banks of the Ohio-New Positions [1:02]	24 Can I Sleep In Your Barn [:50]
6 Mexican Dance [:36]	25 The Scottish Waltz [1:04]
7 Precious Memories [:53]	26 Greensleeves [1:24]
8 Careless Love [:42]	27 Amazing Grace [:49]
9 Bile Dem Cabbage Down [:36]	28 My Wild Irish Rose [:25]
10 Red River Valley [:43]	29 I'll Be All Smiles Tonight [2:15]
11 Clock Wise [:41]	30 Aloha Oe [1:53]
12 Swedish Waltz [:44]	31 Aura Lee [1:08]
13 I'm Thinking Tonight Of My Blue Eyes [:51]	32 Wabash Cannonball [1:01]
14 Waltzing With Brenda [:39]	33 Shenandoah [1:08]
15 Careless Love [1:22]	34 Byrds [1:01]
16 Precious Memories In Harmony [:48]	35 The Great Speckled Bird [2:47]
17 Lovely Maori Girl [1:21]	36 St. Louis Blues [3:02]
18 Wildwood Flower [:40]	37 St. Louis Blues (rhythm track) [3:04]
19 Little Brown Jug [:33]	

The play-along companion CD features a split-track recording which allows the user to boost/mute one track or the other using the stereo balance knob.

Visit us on the Web at http://www.melbay.com — E-mail us at email@melbay.com

2 3 4 5 6 7 8 9 0

TABLE OF CONTENTS

CREDITS
DeWitt Scott—Steel Guitar, St. Louis, MO
Rhythm Tracks—Jimmy Queen, Wentzville, MO
Mixdown—Mike Heath, St. Louis, MO
Mary Scott—Inside Photos, St. Louis, MO

TOOLS OF THE TRADE

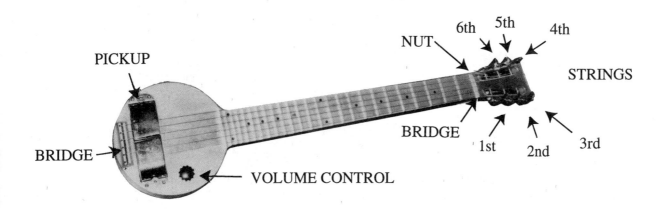

THUMB PICK

THE BAR

Size
3/4 x 2-3/4 "
STAINLESS STEEL

FINGER PICKS

POSITION OF THE THUMB PICK

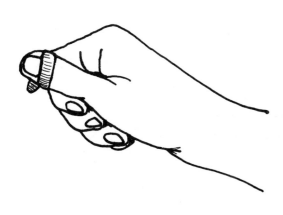

POSITION OF THE FINGER PICKS

THE C6TH TUNING

STRING	OPEN NOTE	GAUGE
1ST	E	.015 PLAIN
2ND	C	.017 PLAIN
3RD	A	.022 PLAIN
4TH	G	.026 PLAIN
5TH	E	.030 WOUND
6TH	C	.036 WOUND

These gauges are just a suggestion. Some players use different gauges.
Some use stainless steel, semi-flat or flat-wound for the wound strings.

Why is the tuning called C6th?

The notes of the tuning correspond to the 1st, 3rd, 5th and 6th notes of the C major scale.

C MAJOR SCALE

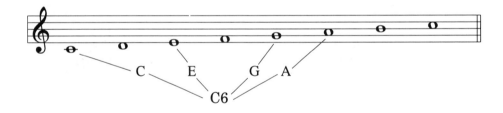

The C6th tuning can also be referred to as "A MINOR 7TH".
1st, 3rd, 5th and 7th notes of an A minor scale.

A MINOR SCALE

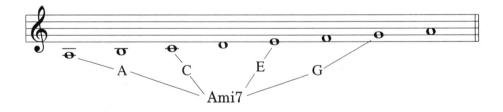

TUNING THE STEEL GUITAR
TUNING TO THE PIANO
Basic Open Tuning
MIDDLE C

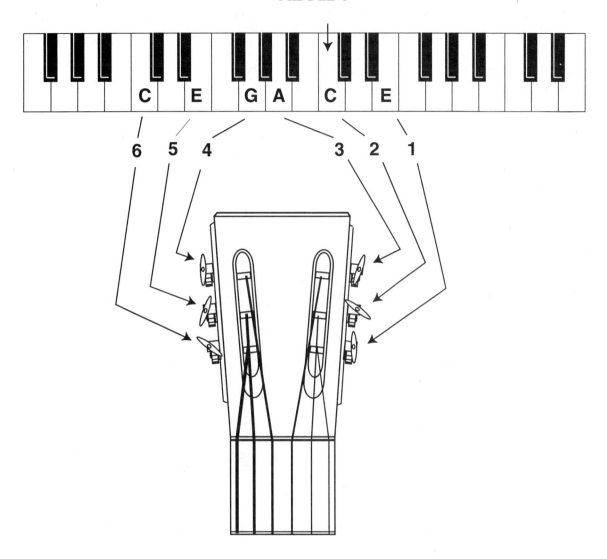

TUNING TO AN ELECTRONIC TUNER USING THE HERTZ SETTINGS

When playing with a band that has keyboards, horns, etc. you can tune your strings to 440 pitch.

When playing with a normal combo band you may want to use the settings listed below.

Strings		Gauges	Meter Settings
1	E	015P	440
2	C	017P	440
3	A	022P	440
4	G	026P	440
5	E	030N	440
6	C	036N	440

Strings		Gauges	Meter Settings
1	E	015P	436.5
2	C	017P	440
3	A	022P	436.5
4	G	026P	440
5	E	030N	436.5
6	C	036N	440

NOTE: N = Rollerwound or semi-flat strings. Flat-wound strings are also popular.

THE RUDIMENTS OF MUSIC

THE STAFF: Music is written on a STAFF consisting of FIVE LINES and FOUR SPACES. The lines and spaces are numbered upward as shown:

```
5TH LINE  ————————————————————————————————————
                            4TH SPACE
4TH LINE  ————————————————————————————————————
                            3RD SPACE
3RD LINE  ————————————————————————————————————
                            2ND SPACE
2ND LINE  ————————————————————————————————————
                            1ST SPACE
1ST LINE  ————————————————————————————————————
```

The lines and spaces are named after letters of the alphabet.

The LINES are named as follows:

The letters can easily be remembered by the sentence — Every Good Boy Does Fine

The letter-names of the SPACES are:

```
4  ——————————————————————————————————
                              E
3  ——————————————————————————————————
                     C
2  ——————————————————————————————————
              A
1  ——————————————————————————————————
       F
```

They spell the word F-A-C-E

The musical alphabet has seven letters — A   B   C   D   E   F   G

The STAFF is divided into measures by vertical lines called BARS

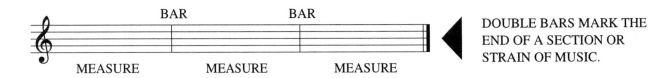

BAR   BAR

MEASURE   MEASURE   MEASURE

DOUBLE BARS MARK THE END OF A SECTION OR STRAIN OF MUSIC.

THE CLEF:

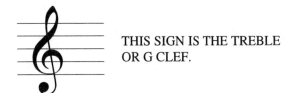

THIS SIGN IS THE TREBLE OR G CLEF.

THE SECOND LINE OF THE TREBLE CLEF IS KNOWN AS THE G LINE. MANY PEOPLE CALL THE TREBLE CLEF THE G CLEF BECAUSE IT CIRCLES AROUND THE G LINE.

ALL GUITAR MUSIC WILL BE WRITTEN IN THIS CLEF.

NOTES:

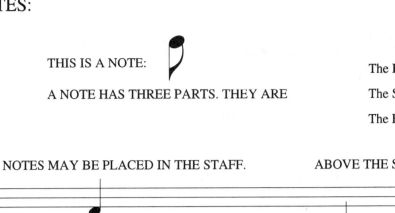

THIS IS A NOTE:

A NOTE HAS THREE PARTS. THEY ARE

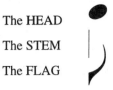

The HEAD

The STEM

The FLAG

NOTES MAY BE PLACED IN THE STAFF.   ABOVE THE STAFF.

AND BELOW THE STAFF.

A note will bear the name of the line or space it occupies on the staff.
The location of a note in, above or below the staff will indicate the Pitch.

PITCH: the height or depth of a tone.

TONE: a musical sound.

TYPES OF NOTES

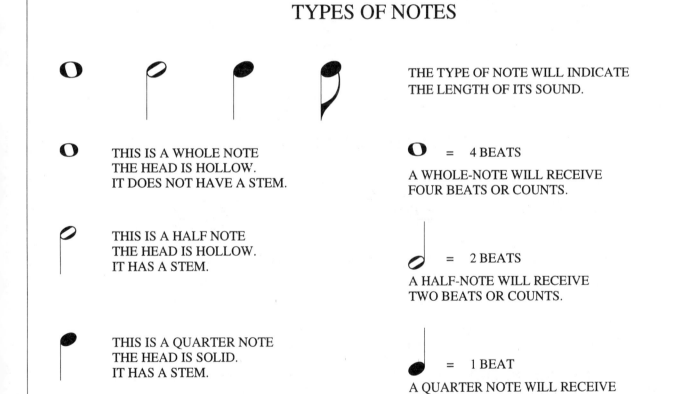

THE TYPE OF NOTE WILL INDICATE
THE LENGTH OF ITS SOUND.

THIS IS A WHOLE NOTE
THE HEAD IS HOLLOW.
IT DOES NOT HAVE A STEM.

O = 4 BEATS

A WHOLE-NOTE WILL RECEIVE
FOUR BEATS OR COUNTS.

THIS IS A HALF NOTE
THE HEAD IS HOLLOW.
IT HAS A STEM.

= 2 BEATS

A HALF-NOTE WILL RECEIVE
TWO BEATS OR COUNTS.

THIS IS A QUARTER NOTE
THE HEAD IS SOLID.
IT HAS A STEM.

= 1 BEAT

A QUARTER NOTE WILL RECEIVE
ONE BEAT OR COUNT.

THIS IS AN EIGHTH NOTE
THE HEAD IS SOLID.
IT HAS A STEM AND A FLAG.

= 1/2 BEAT

AN EIGHTH-NOTE WILL RECEIVE ONE-HALF
BEAT OR COUNT. (2 FOR 1 BEAT)

RESTS:

A REST is a sign used to designate a period of silence.
This period of silence will be of the same duration of time as the note to which it corresponds.

 THIS IS AN EIGHTH REST   THIS IS A QUARTER REST

 THIS IS A HALF REST. NOTE THAT IT LAYS ON THE LINE.

 THIS IS A WHOLE REST. NOTE THAT IT HANGS DOWN FROM THE LINE.

NOTES

WHOLE 4 COUNTS	HALF 2 COUNTS	QUARTER 1 COUNT	EIGHTH 2 FOR 1 COUNT

RESTS

THE TIME SIGNATURE

THE ABOVE EXAMPLES ARE THE COMMON TYPES OF TIME SIGNATURES TO BE USED IN THIS BOOK.

$\dfrac{4}{4}$ THE TOP NUMBER INDICATES THE NUMBER OF BEATS PER MEASURE.

$\dfrac{4}{4}$ BEATS PER MEASURE

$\dfrac{4}{4}$ THE BOTTOM NUMBER INDICATES THE TYPE OF NOTE RECEIVING ONE BEAT.

$\dfrac{4}{4}$ A QUARTER-NOTE RECEIVES ONE BEAT

 SIGNIFIES SO CALLED "COMMON TIME" AND IS SIMPLY ANOTHER WAY OF DESIGNATING $\frac{4}{4}$ TIME.

TABLATURE INSTRUCTIONS

7   A single number receives the same count as a quarter note.

7 7   Receive 1/ 2 count as in eighth notes.

7. 7   Dotted quarter tied to a eighth note.

$\lceil 3 \rceil$
7 7 7   Triplets. Receives one count.

–   Designates either a rest of one count or sustain for one count.

– –   Designates either a rest of two counts or sustain for two counts.

– – –   Designates either a rest of three counts or sustain for three counts.

/   Gliss sign. (Glissando). Pick the first note and slide to the second note. Example: 6 / 7 Pick the 6 and slide to the 7. DO NOT PICK THE 7!

~~~~~   Sustain (let the notes ring for the duration of the sign).

◡   Slide into the designated fret. Example: ◡9 Slide from the 8th or 8 1/2 fret.

⦙   Strum. Strum all the strings with the thumb or strum the lower notes with the thumb and the top note with the first finger.

[: :]   Repeat signs. Repeat the measures that are between these signs.

⌐1.   1st Ending. Play this ending and then go back to the "other" repeat sign. Play from the "other" repeat sign and skip the 1st ending and play the 2nd ending.

Har - -   The harmonic is the pleasant high pitch sound that is produced by substituting the use of the bar with the palm of the right hand. This is executed by placing the palm either 5 FRETS, 7 FRETS or 12 FRETS above the bar. When placing the palm on the string (or strings) treat it as it were a hot stove! Place the palm very lightly on the string, pick the required note and then raise your palm very quickly! If the bar is located on the 3rd fret the palm of the hand is on the same string, but up 12 frets (Fret 15). Or 5 or 7 frets up as indicated on the tablature.

F.H. - -   Finger Harmonics. Executed the same way as Har- -, but substituting the tip of the 4th finger instead of the plam.

K.H. - -   Knuckle Harmonics. Executed the same as F.H., but, substituting the knuckle or the 3rd or 4th finger of the right hand. This method is not used in this course but is something you should be aware of as it is widely used by many players.

0 1 0
x x   Mordent. Also called Hammer - On and Pull-Off. Pick the first 0 then quickly lay the bar on the 1st fret letting the bar sound the note and then "Pull Off" the bar quickly sounding the 0 fret.

Listening to the recording accompanying this book will be a great help in understanding the above symbols!

BLOCKING AND RIGHT-HAND POSITIONS
EXERCISE

PICK BLOCKING: Method #1.

Lay the 3rd finger of your picking hand along the side of the 2nd finger. As the 2nd finger picks the string the 3rd finger is there to touch that string and block the note from sustaining. A difficult procedure but one that is widely used by the Pro's.

The thumb is used to block the string you play.

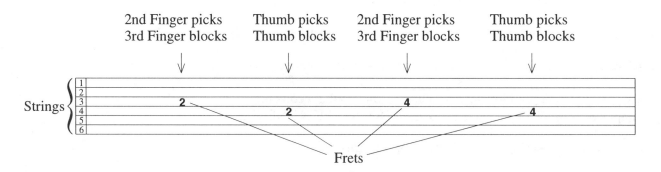

PALM BLOCKING: Method #2.

The 3rd and 4th fingers of the right hand are tucked underneath the palm of the hand, blocking the note the thumb plays with the palm of the hand. The note that is picked with the finger can be blocked with the knuckle of the 3rd finger.

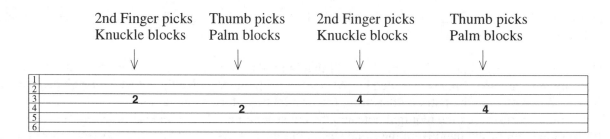

Right Hand
Ring and little finger are tucked under
with the fingers blocking the treble strings
and the palm blocking the bass strings.

Right Hand
3rd finger lying next to the
2nd finger.

BLOCKING EXERCISES
(For best results play these exercises EVERY DAY and play each one over and over and over!)

E Major Scale

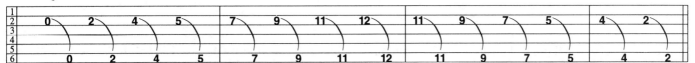

Whole Tones

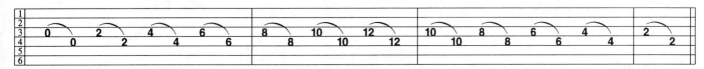

Diminished

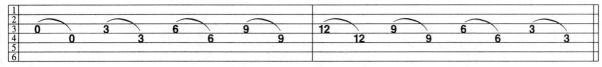

Augmented

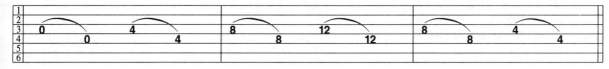

Interval of 4th

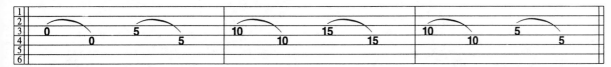

THE VIBRATO

The pretty oscillating sound produced by moving
(or rolling) the bar above and below the fret.

The vibrato is a personal thing. The amount of vibrato used helps establish your own tone. The real fast vibrato suggests the Hawaiian style. The slower rolling motion suggests the more modern style of playing. Whichever method you choose, first establish a true note before you start the vibrato. The vibrato also helps you to sustain the notes.

STYLE #ONE

Back and forward motion

3rd fret

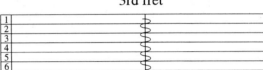

The "back and forward motion". The bar is centered over the fret - the ring & little finger are anchored on the strings behind the bar. This assures that you will stay in tune, move the bar about 1/4 inch above the fret and about 1/4 inch below the fret. How fast or slow you move the bar is determined by you.

STYLE #TWO

Rolling motion

The "rolling motion". The bar is centered over the fret - the ring and little finger can be anchored or suspended above the strings. Now, instead of moving the bar back and forwards, simply roll the bar back and forth. This style is more effective on slow tunes. Fast tunes sometimes require no vibrato at all.

NOTES C, D AND E

Keep the bar directly above the fret.
Keep the right hand in its proper position.

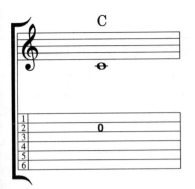

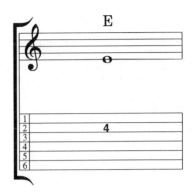

Whole Notes

A Whole Note (𝅝) Receives Four Beats

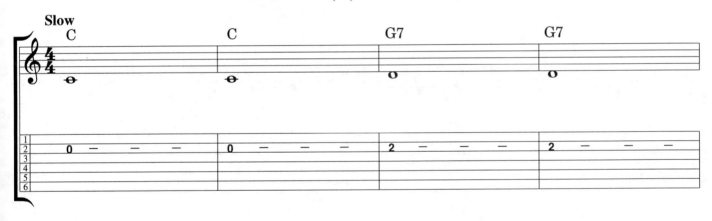

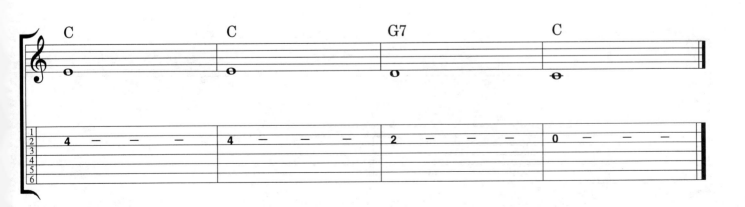

13

Half Notes

A half-notes (♩) receives two beats

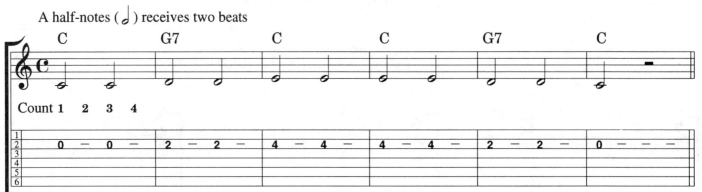

Quarter Notes

A quarter-note (♩) receives one beat

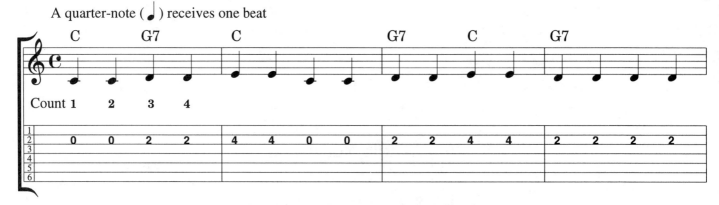

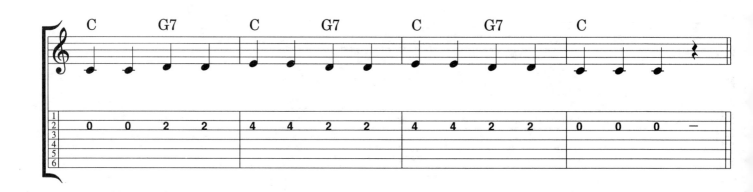

The Mixmaster

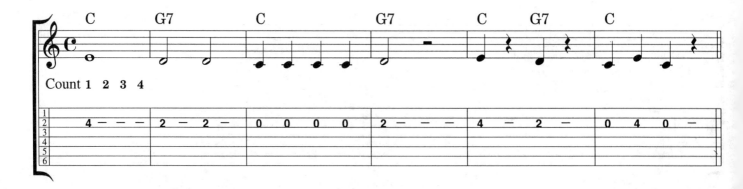

SIDEWALKS OF NASHVILLE

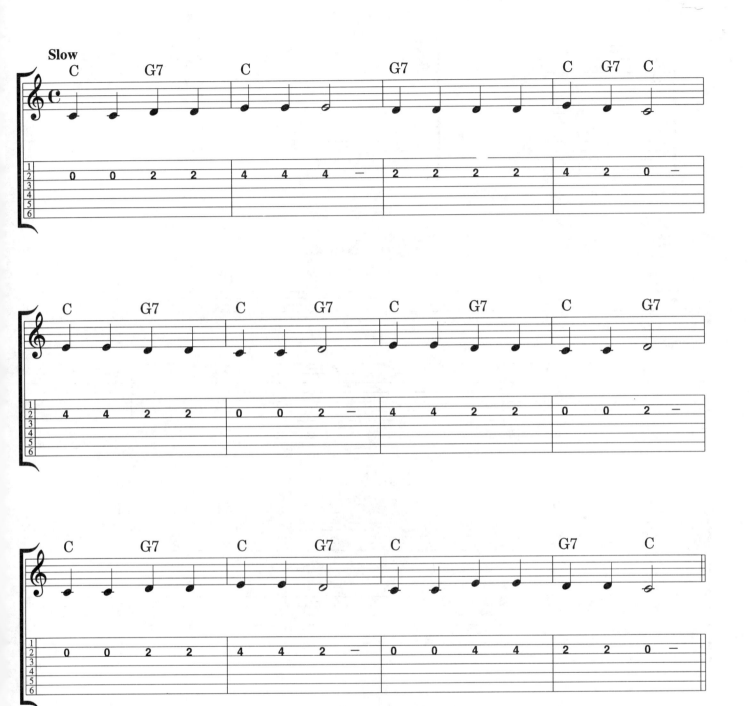

THE NOTES F, G AND A

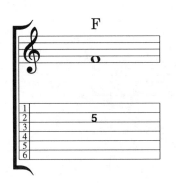

Whole Notes

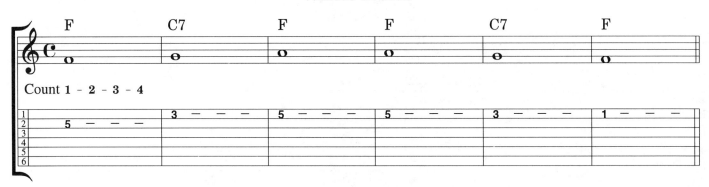

Half Notes

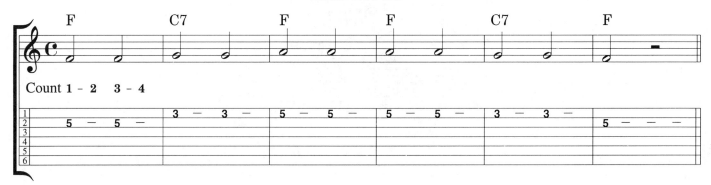

Quarter Notes

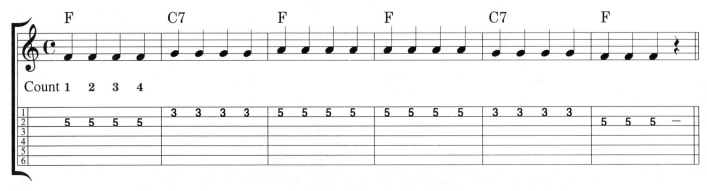

SANDY ANN

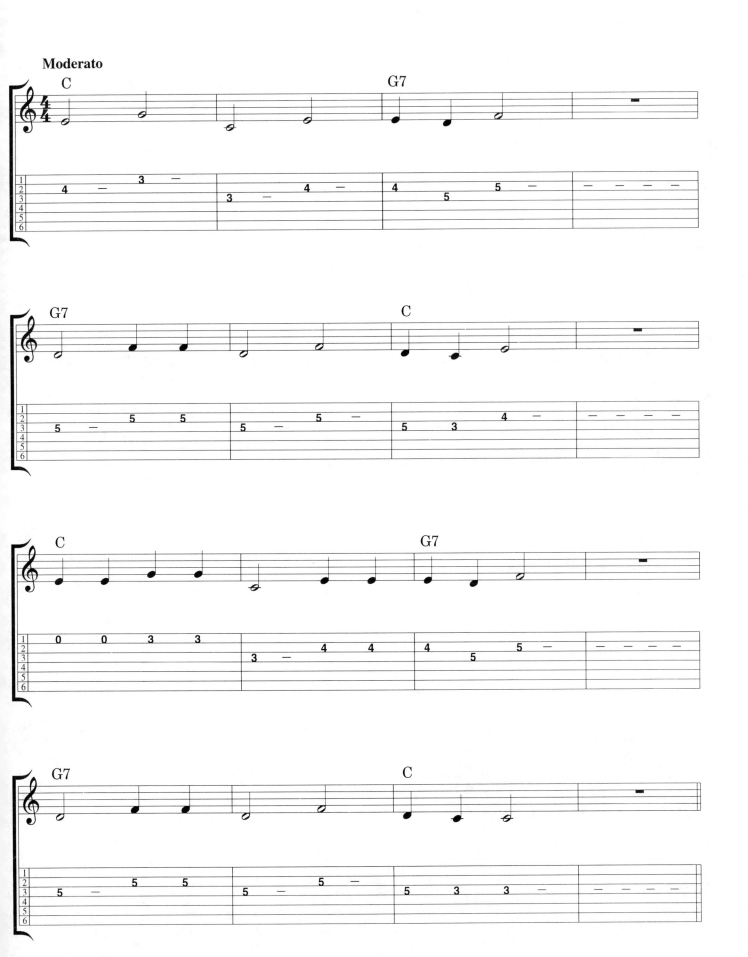

BANKS OF THE OHIO

Start here

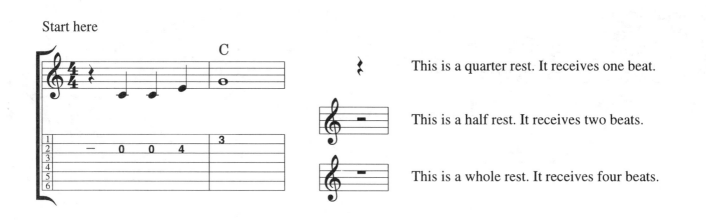

This is a quarter rest. It receives one beat.

This is a half rest. It receives two beats.

This is a whole rest. It receives four beats.

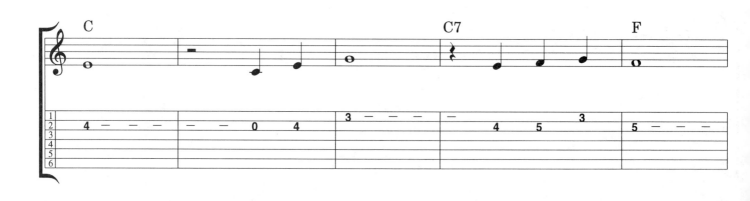

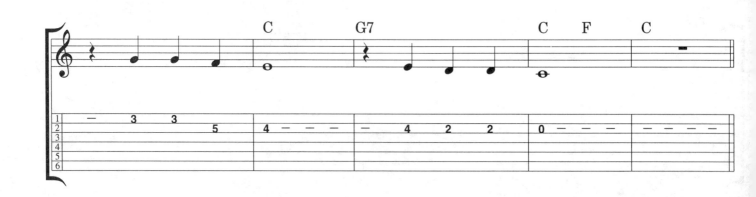

BANKS OF THE OHIO

ALTERNATE SINGLE NOTE POSITIONS
(Learning these alternatives will make your playing come easier.)

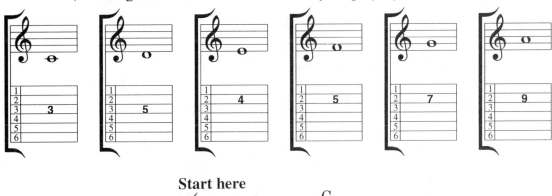

Start here

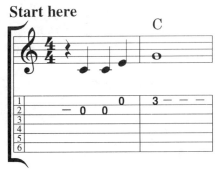

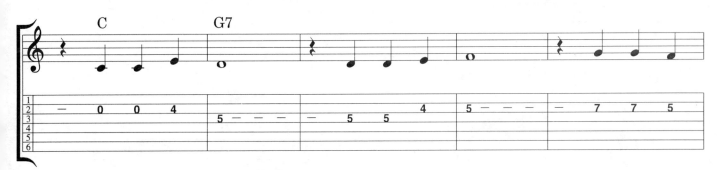

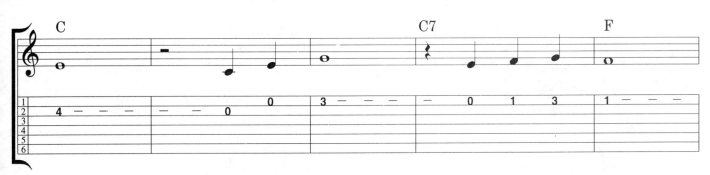

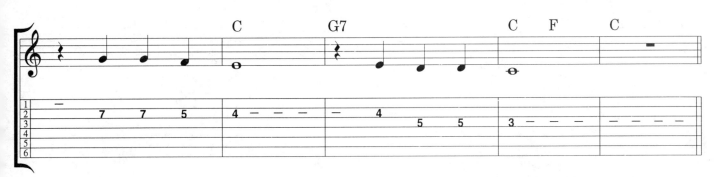

THREE - FOUR TIME

3 = Beats per measure.

4 = Type of note receiving one beat (quarter note).

Remember: In three-four time, we will have three beats per measure.

A quarter note will receive one beat.

MEXICAN DANCE

THE RULE OF THE DOT

A dot placed after a note or a rest increases its time value by one half.

Examples

𝅗𝅥 = 2 counts   𝅗𝅥. = 3 counts

♩ = 1 counts   ♩. = 1 1/2 counts

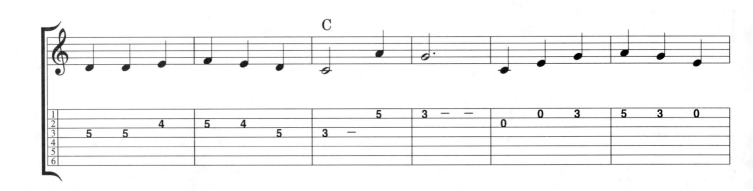

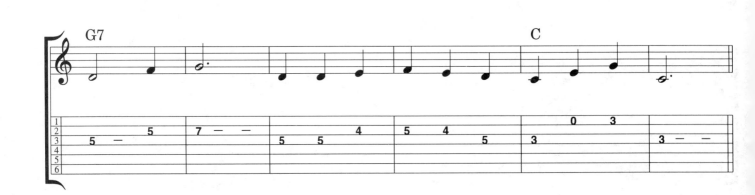

NOTES B, C, D AND E

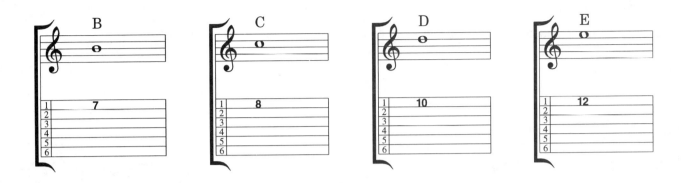

A STUDY

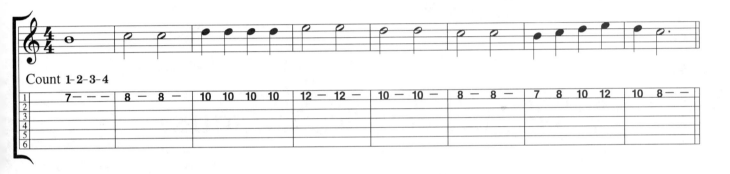

Count 1-2-3-4

PRECIOUS MEMORIES

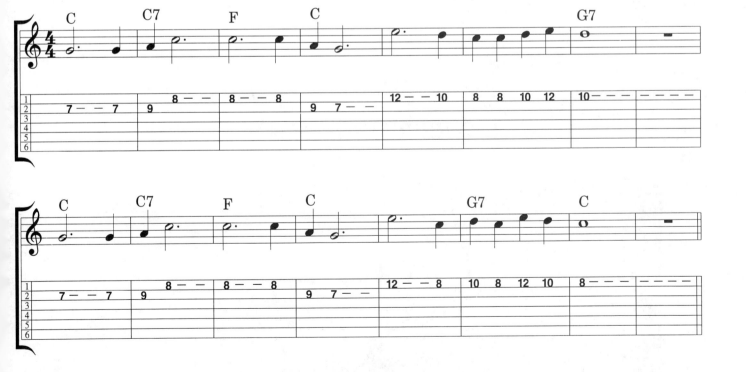

21

THE TIE

The tie is a curved line between two notes of the same pitch.
The first note is played and held for the time duration of both. The second note is not played but held.

Example

Count 1- 2- 3   1- 2- 3
                      (Hold)

INTRODUCING THREE NEW NOTES

Ledger lines = Lines added above or below the staff

THEIR LOCATION

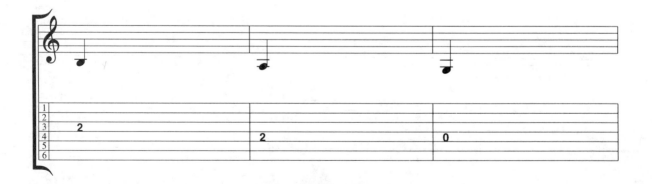

22

CARELESS LOVE

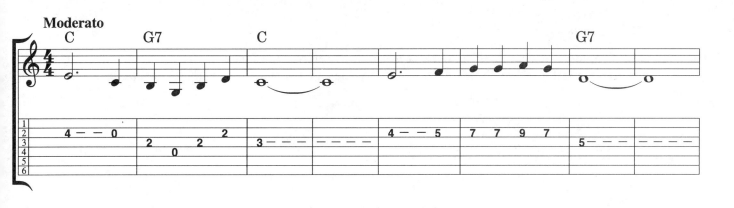

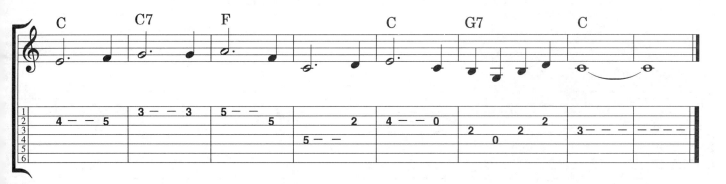

BILE DEM CABBAGE DOWN

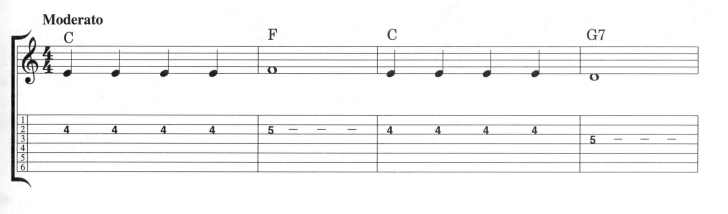

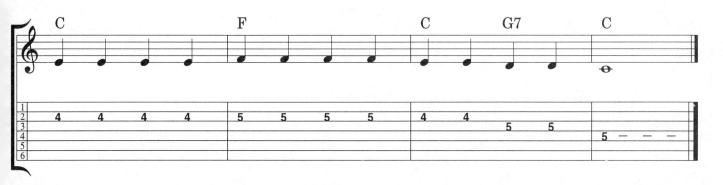

PICK - UP NOTES

The notes at the beginning of a strain before the first measure are referred to as pick-up notes. The rhythm for pick-up notes is taken from the last measure of the selection and the beats are counted as such. (Note the two beats in the last measure.)

RED RIVER VALLEY

Arranged by DeWitt Scott

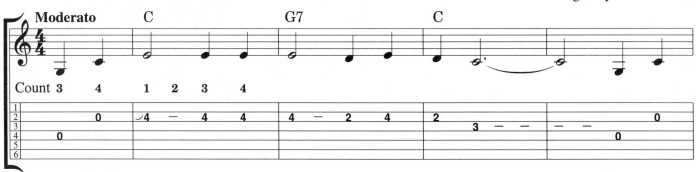

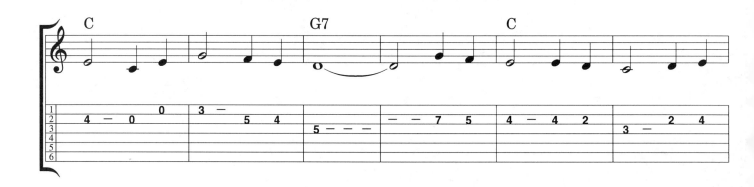

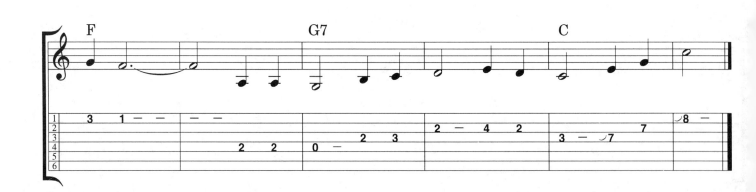

THE E AND G, F AND A, G AND B NOTES

AND THEIR LOCATIONS

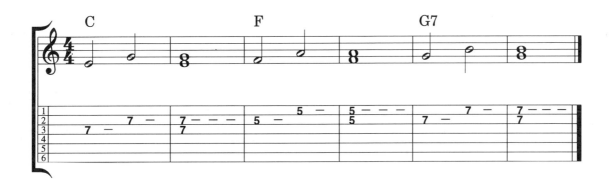

TWO NOTE EXCERCISE

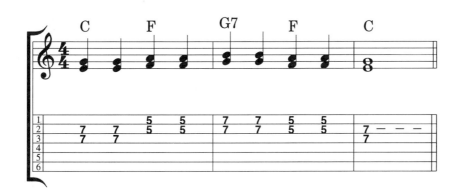

WHEN TWO OR MORE NOTES ARE WRITTEN
ON THE SAME STEM PLAY THEM SIMULTANEOUSLY

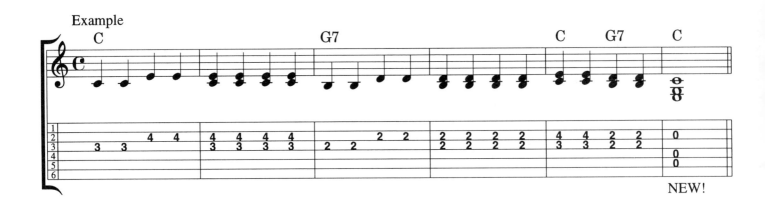

CLOCK WISE

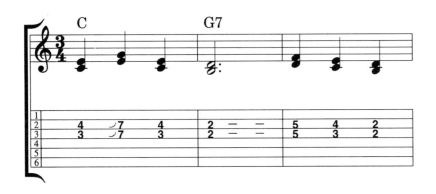

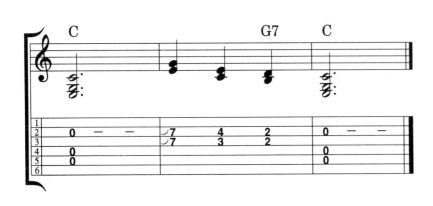

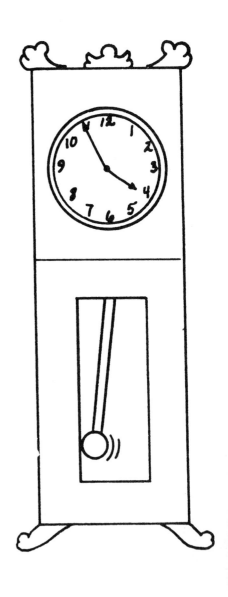

HARMONY IN SIXTH'S

Fingering = Thumb plays the lower note - 2nd finger plays the higher note.

Exercise #1

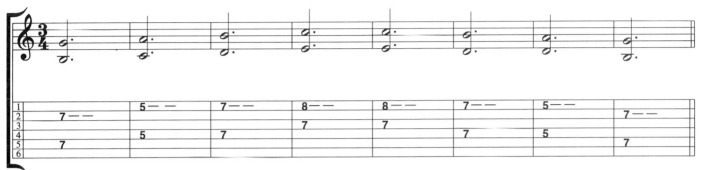

(See page 96 for slant bar instructions)

Exercise #2

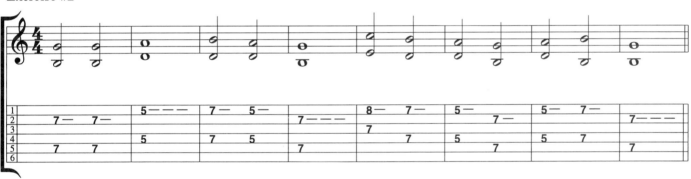

This exercise is called "intervals of a sixth" for this reason;
(The distance from the lower note to the higher note is six notes.)

Examples

B to G = Ⓑ C D E F Ⓖ   D to B = Ⓓ E F G A Ⓑ
         ① 2 3 4 5 ⑥   ① 2 3 4 5 ⑥

C to A = Ⓒ D E F G Ⓐ   G to E = Ⓖ A B C D Ⓔ
         ① 2 3 4 5 ⑥   ① 2 3 4 5 ⑥

SWEDISH WALTZ

THIRDS AND SIXTHS IN ALTERNATE POSITIONS

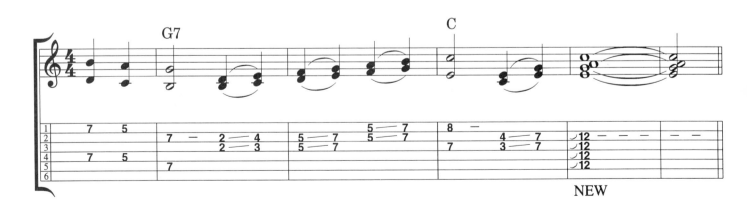

NEW

I'M THINKING TONIGHT OF MY BLUE EYES

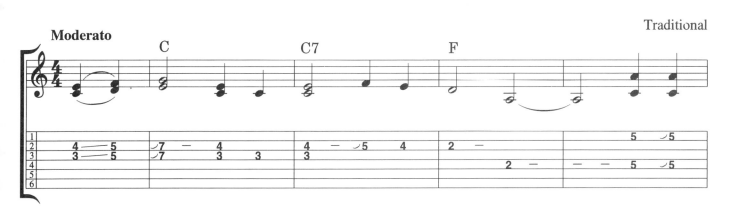

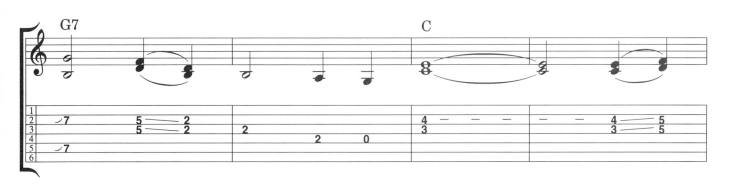

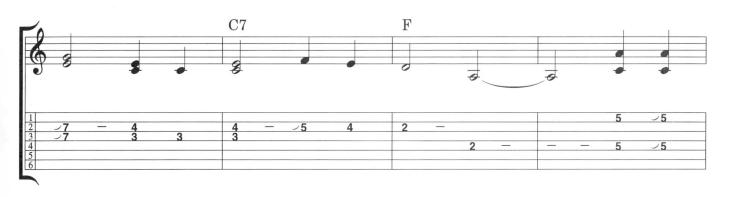

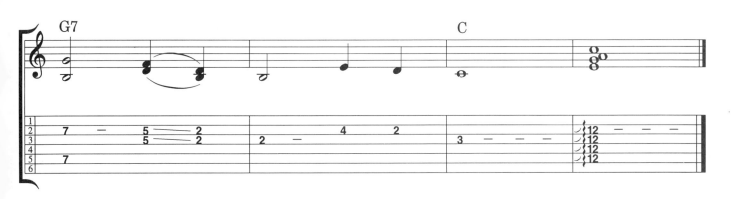

CHORDS

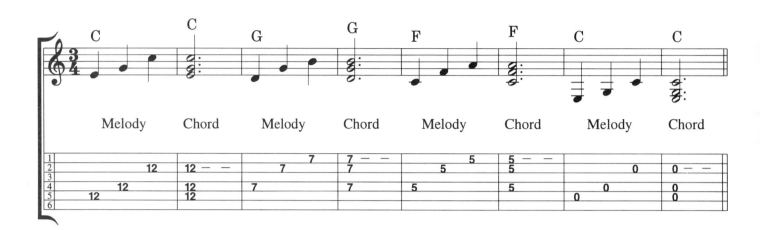

A melody is succession of single tones.
A chord is a combination of tones sounded together.

THREE STRING WALTZ

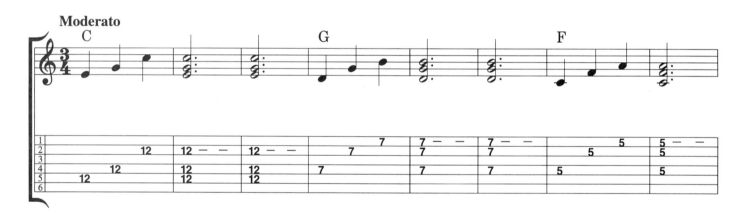

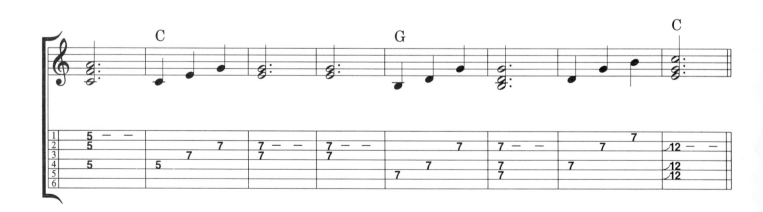

30

MORE ON BLOCKING

Blocking is the separating of each note — not allowing them to ring from one note to another. This technique will be essential in the fast exercises that will be used later.

Style one: Keep the little finger of the right hand extended and block with the flat side of the hand.

Style two: Tuck the third and fourth fingers of the right hand under and block with the knuckles and the heel of the hand.

Style three: Block with the picks.

WALTZING WITH BRENDA

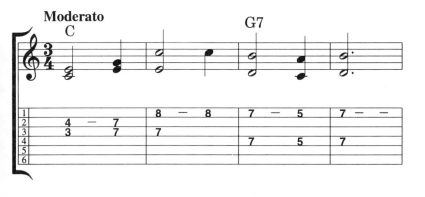

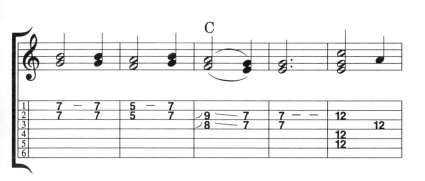

SOME NICE RUNS AND FILLS

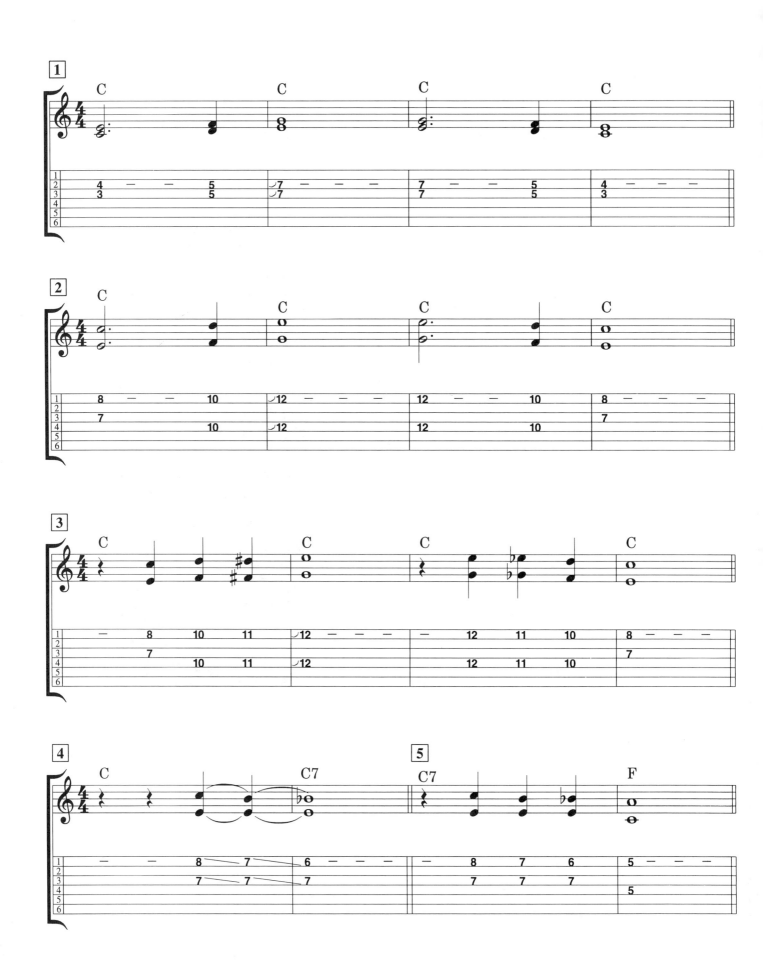

MORE RUNS AND FILLS

MORE RUNS AND FILLS

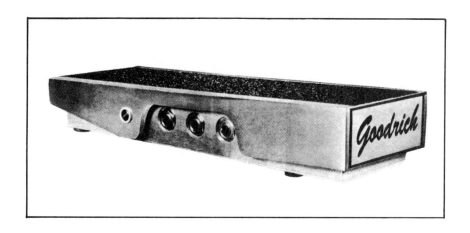

VOLUME PEDAL

The number one objective is to control the picking of the steel guitar in a similar manner as on a Spanish guitar. Once you have gained control of your picking and all of the notes of a chord are balanced (and your single note passages are clean and clear), it is time to start using your foot volume pedal. This pedal is simply a remote volume control that you use with your right foot. A good "rule of thumb" to start off with is to always keep the volume on at a minimum level and do not go any lower than that preset volume. Use your pedal to keep that volume level the same. When the volume begins to fade, push the pedal down to bring the desired level back up. Do not be completely dependent on the pedal to cover up your bad notes and do not constantly pump the pedal. With practice, the volume pedal becomes a part of your personality. It will be very essential in the expression and execution of your music. This is especially true on slow tunes. The pedal is rarely used on fast tunes.

FIRST AND SECOND ENDINGS

Sometimes two endings are required in certain selections. One to lead back into a repeated chorus and one to close it.

They will be shown like this.

The first time play the bracketed ending 1. Repeat from the beginning. The second time skip the first ending and play ending no. 2.

CARELESS LOVE

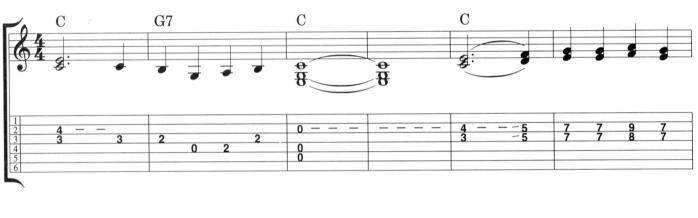

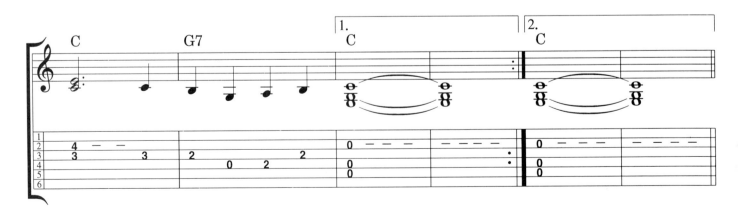

♯SHARPS, ♭FLATS, AND ♮NATURALS

THE DISTANCE FROM ONE FRET TO THE NEXT IS A HALF STEP. TWO HALF STEPS MAKE A WHOLE STEP.

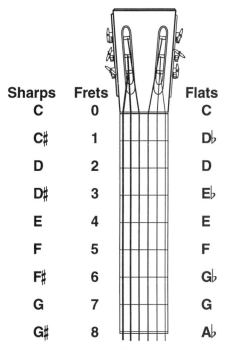

Sharps	Frets	Flats
C	0	C
C♯	1	D♭
D	2	D
D♯	3	E♭
E	4	E
F	5	F
F♯	6	G♭
G	7	G
G♯	8	A♭

Notes are based on the 2nd string.

HALF STEPS ARE ONE FRET APART   WHOLE STEPS ARE TWO FRETS APART

ENHARMONIC = Notes that are written differently but sound the same.

 SHARPS ♯ RAISE THE NOTE A HALF STEP. PLAY
THE NEXT FRET HIGHER.

FLATS ♭ LOWER THE NOTE A HALF STEP.
PLAY THE NEXT FRET LOWER.

NATURALS ♮ CANCEL A PREVIOUS ♯ OR ♭ .

♯ SHARPS, ♭ FLATS, AND ♮ NATURALS

The Sharp ♯   THE SHARP PLACED BEFORE A NOTE RAISES ITS PITCH 1/2 - STEP OR ONE FRET.

The Flat ♭   THE FLAT PLACED BEFORE A NOTE LOWERS ITS PITCH 1/2 - STEP OR ONE FRET.

The Natural ♮   THE NATURAL RESTORES A NOTE TO ITS NORMAL POSITION. IT CANCELS ALL ACCIDENTALS PREVIOUSLY USED IN THAT PARTICULAR MEASURE.

CHROMATICS

The alteration of the pitches of tones is brought about by the use of symbols called CHROMATICS.
(Also referred to as ACCIDENTALS)

CHROMATICS ASCENDING IN SHARPS

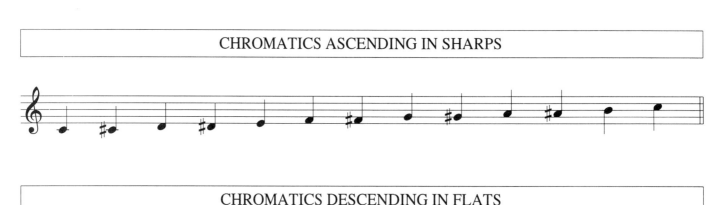

CHROMATICS DESCENDING IN FLATS

EXERCISE WITH SHARPS

Start slow (andante) and learn to play it fast (allegro)

When a sharp (♯) or flat (♭) appears in a measure it is called an accidental and remains in effect for that measure only.

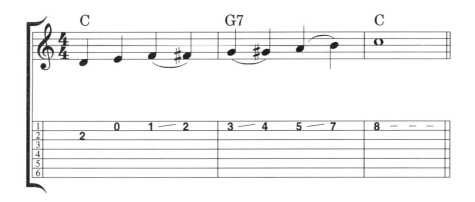

SAME RUN - DIFFERENT POSITION

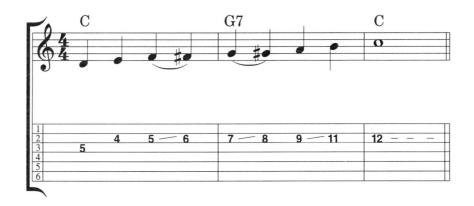

EXERCISE WITH FLATS

Start slow (andante) and learn to play it fast (allegro)

When a sharp (♯) or flat (♭) appears in a measure it is called an accidental and remains in effect for that measure only.

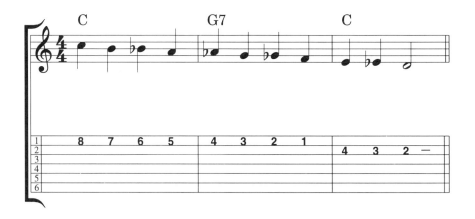

SAME RUN - DIFFERENT POSITION

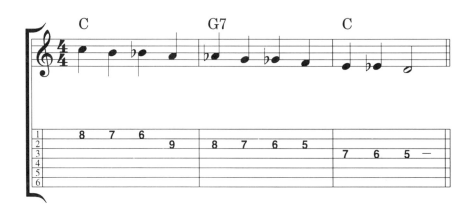

PRECIOUS MEMORIES

A STEEL GUITAR SOLO

Traditional

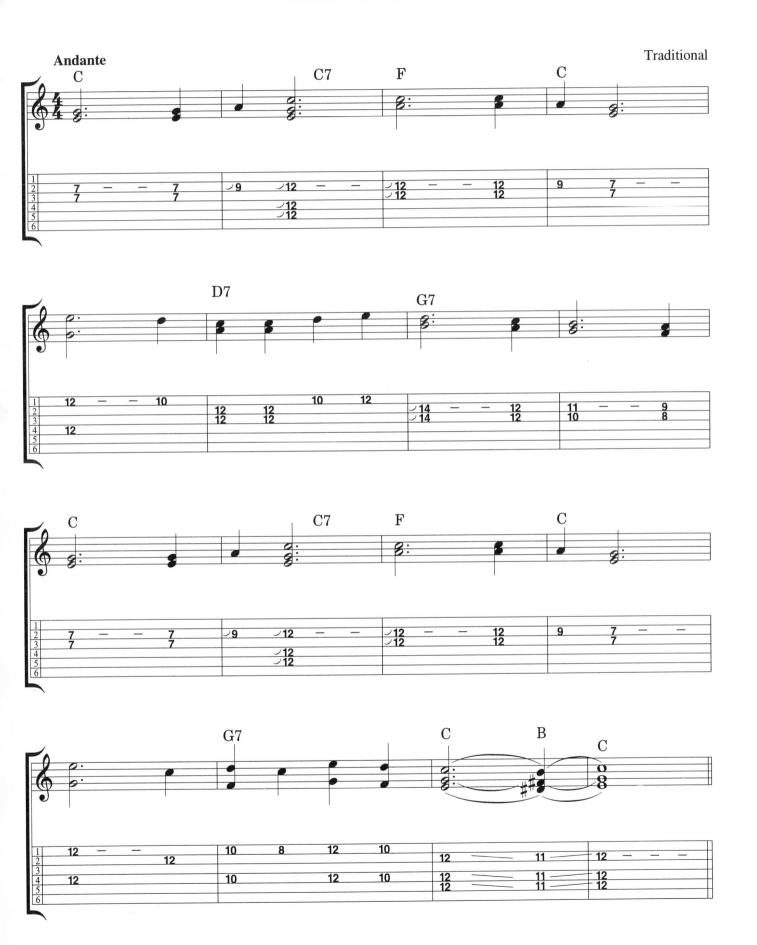

LOVELY MAORI GIRL

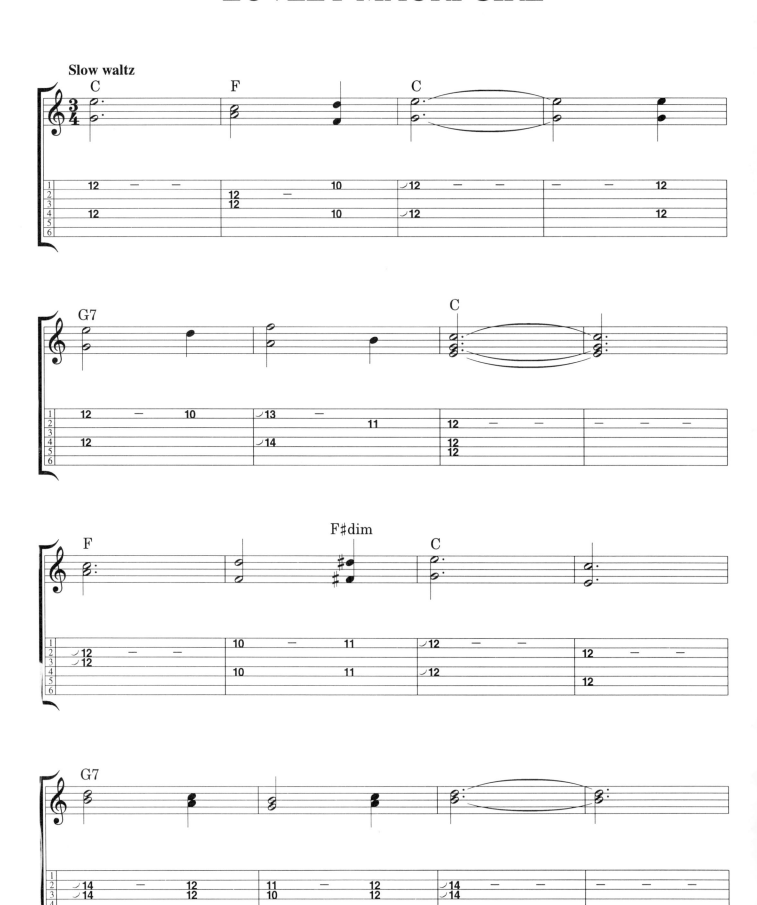

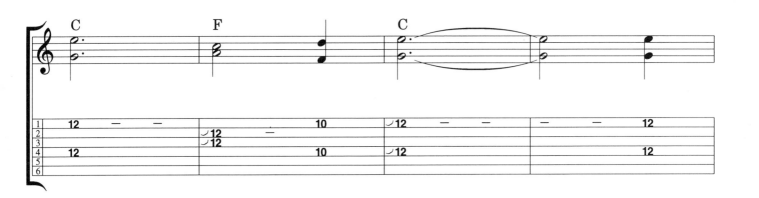

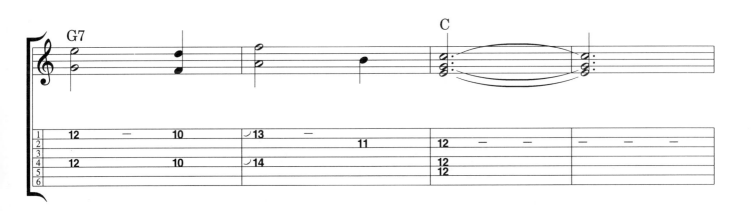

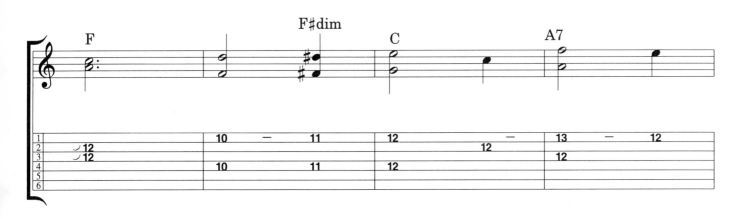

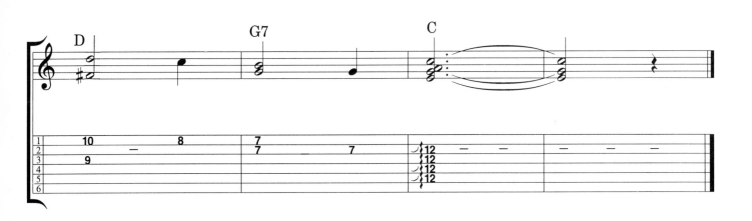

THE EIGHTH NOTE

An eighth note receives one - half beat. (One quarter note equals two eighth notes.)

An eighth note will have a head, stem, and flag. If two or more notes are in successive order they may be connected by a beam. (See example)

EIGHTH NOTES AND EIGHTH RESTS

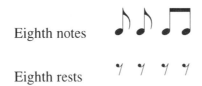

Eighth notes

Eighth rests

THE SCALE IN EIGHTH NOTES

Count 1 & 2 & 3 & 4 &   1 & 2 & 3 & 4 &   1 & 2 & 3   4

EIGHTH NOTE EXERCISE

The Mordent. All numbers with the X underneath them are NOT TO BE PICKED. Lay the bar on that fret (or off of it) letting the bar sound it. Referred to as "Hammer-On" and "Pull-Off".

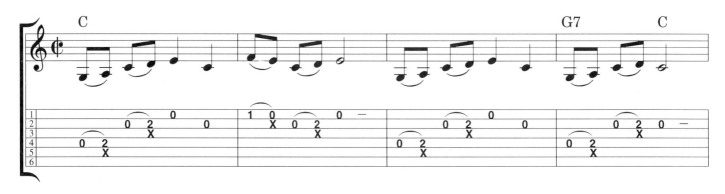

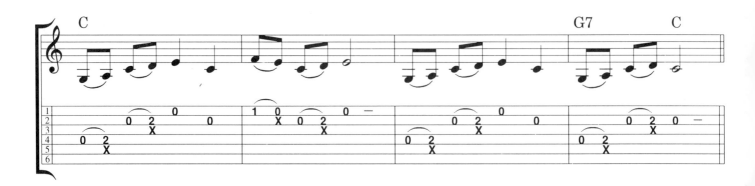

WILDWOOD FLOWER

LITTLE BROWN JUG

Traditional

THE MAJOR SCALE

The major scale has eight notes. They are in alphabetical order. They follow this pattern:

Whole Step								
Whole Step								
Half	OR	1	1	1/2	1	1	1	1/2
Whole Step								
Whole Step								
Whole Step								
Half								

Whole Step = Two Frets

Half Step = One Fret

EXAMPLE
C Scale

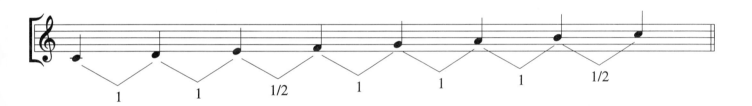

An aid in memorizing this pattern - there are two places where you have 1/2 steps (or one fret apart) They are from E to F and from B to C. All others are a whole step apart (Two frets). The C scale starts on C (also called the root) and ends on C.

C SCALE ON THE STEEL GUITAR ONE STRING

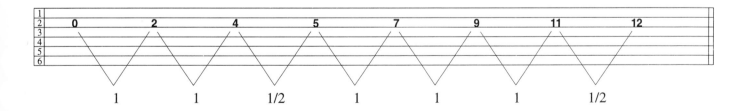

HALF SCALE EXERCISE FORM NUMBER ONE

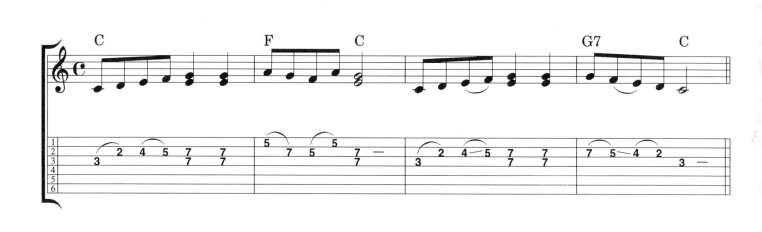

HALF SCALE EXERCISE FORM NUMBER TWO

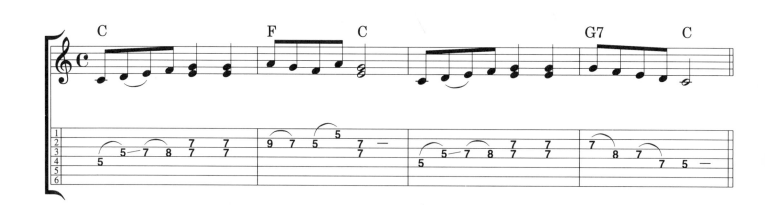

HALF SCALE EXERCISE FORM NUMBER THREE

THE C SCALE HARMONIZED

C SCALE POSITION #ONE

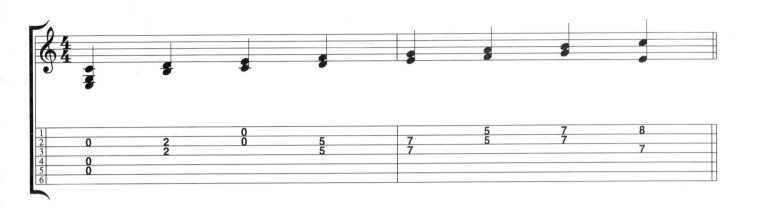

C SCALE POSITION #TWO

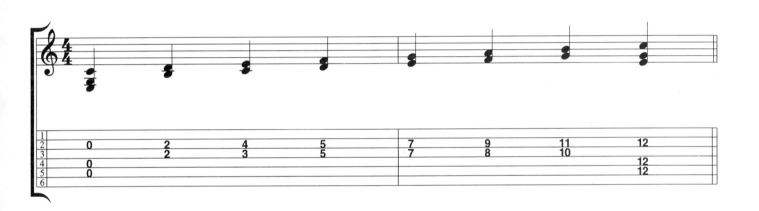

The major scale consists of eight notes in alphabetical order.

C Scale

| C | D | E | F | G | A | B | C |

They also can be numbered - one thru eight.

C Scale

| 1 | 2 | 3 | 4 | 5 | 6 | 7 | 8 |
| (C) | (D) | (E) | (F) | (G) | (A) | (B) | (C) |

JOY TO THE WORLD
Notice C Scale First Eight Notes (in Reverse)

Traditional

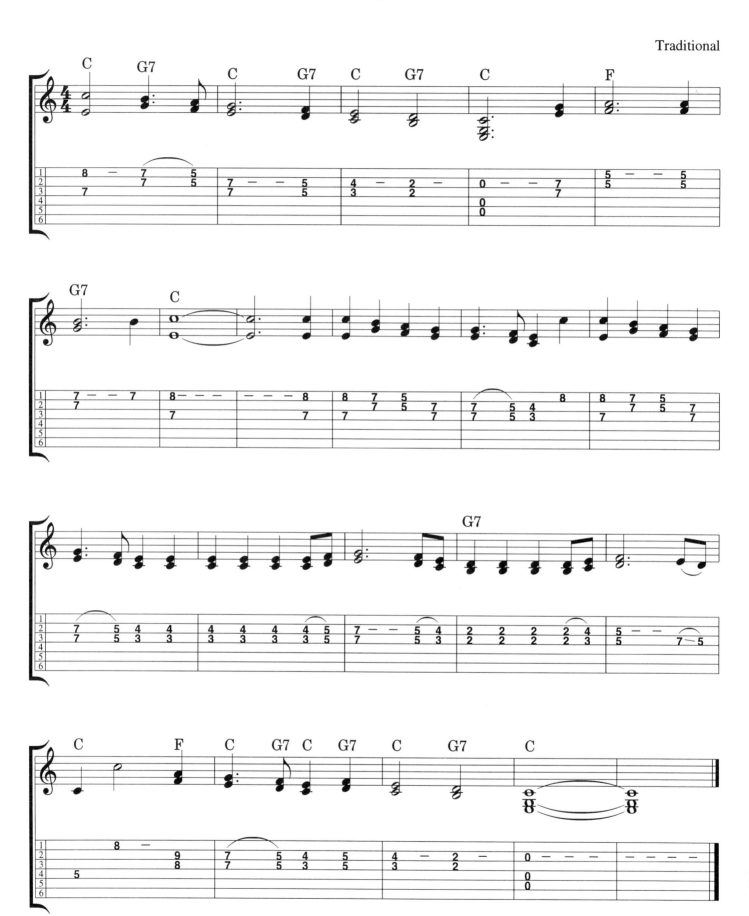

SINGLE NOTE SCALE EXERCISES

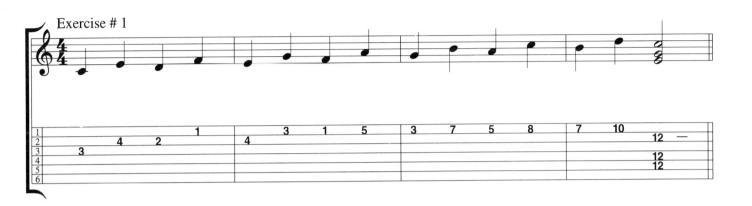

Exercise # 1

NOTE: It is possible to play your steel guitar is such a way to make it <u>difficult</u> instead of <u>easy!</u> You may be musically correct but you also may be complicating your playing. Exercise #1 is musically correct BUT <u>complicates</u> your playing and could take some of the fun out of your practice time. True, you may benefit from the "blocking" required to play it, but that is not all there is to playing the steel guitar.

Now try Exercise #2. It is more realistic and lays the notes in easy order. If you think "This is easy" that's OK but remember, "THERE IS NO EASY WAY TO PLAY THE STEEL GUITAR!" It takes a lot of practice and more importantly "IT TAKES A LOT OF DEDICATION!"

Exercise # 2

Exercise # 3

THREE PRINCIPAL CHORDS

As a tune is being performed, the basic rule for its chord changes are: the first note of the scale, the fourth note of the scale and the fifth note of the scale.

Example using the C Scale

C	D	E	F	G	A	B
1st			4th	5th		

So the three principal chord changes in the key of C are:

C	F	and	G

It can be referred to as

1	4	and	5

As you progress in this book and gain more musical knowledge there will be some changes to the rules. One, for example, is that the 5 will change to 5^{7th}. Other chords will be added to the "Basic Rule" as well as chord substitutions.

NOTE : Traditional musicians use Roman Numerals I, IV, V.

NASHVILLE NUMBER SYSTEM

By using the numbers 1-4-5 as a substitute for the notes of the C major scale you in essence are using the number system! The number system was originated by session recording musicians so when a singer would change keys they would not have to rewrite their chord charts. They realized if the notes would change from one key to another the numbers would remain the same regardless of what key they had to play in. They would simply "mentally" make the change.

EXAMPLE:

Key of C				Key of G		
C	F	G7		G	C	D7
1	4	5		1	4	5

Notice the notes changed when the key was changed BUT the numbers remained the same!

MAJOR CHORDS

The formula for construction of the major chord is:

1   3   5

Meaning the 1st note of the scale, the 3rd note of the scale

and the 5th note of the scale.

therefore

C   E   and   G   are a C major chord

Example

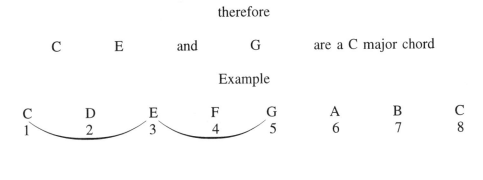

C	D	E	F	G	A	B	C
1	2	3	4	5	6	7	8

The   F   Chord

F   A   C

compiled from the F major scale.

The   G   Chord

G   B   D

compiled from the G major scale.

It's true we have not studied the F or G major scales as yet, but we can use them in our studies as they are part of the three principal chord changes in the key of C. We will now discuss them in their useable forms.

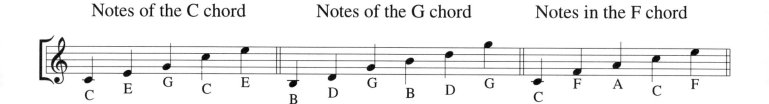

Notes of the C chord   Notes of the G chord   Notes in the F chord

C E G C E   B D G B D G   C F A C F

NOTES OF THE C-F-G CHORD HARMONIZED

One Position   Another Position

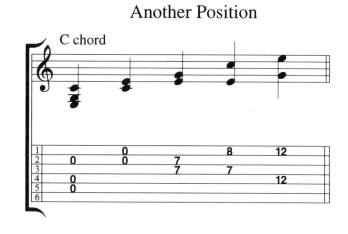

NOTES OF THE F CHORD HARMONIZED

One Position   Another Position

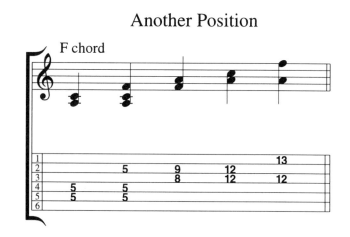

NOTES OF THE G CHORD HARMONIZED

One Position   Another Position

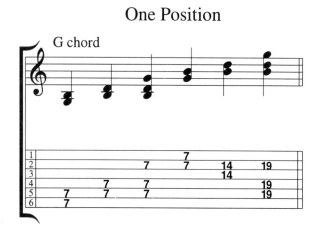

TWO POSITION TUNE

Don't let the two positions fool you-This tune shows two ways of playing the same notes-You learned both in the major scale positions and the major chord positions. Look at the chord first, then the melody.

TWO POSITION TUNE

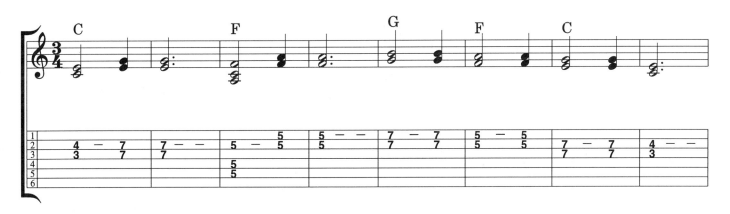

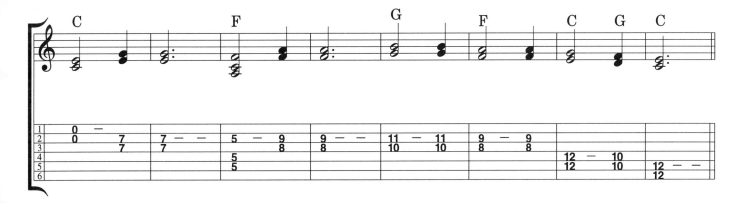

NOTES OR NUMBERS?

If you have learned your notes, scales, and chords, you can play off some sheet music in the key of C. For supplementary material take a sheet of music, play the correct notes and observe the correct timing and you should be pleasantly surprised!

FURTHER EXPLANATION OF
THE "C," "F" AND "G" CHORDS

Upon strict study of the C chord in harmony you will find only the notes C-E and G.
Also, when you take a close look at the F chord in harmony, you will find only the F-A and C notes.
The same with the G chord-only G-B and D notes.

ROOT OF THE CHORD

The 1st note of a major scale is also called "Root".

Examples:

The Root of the C chord is C.
The Root of the F chord is F.
The Root of the G chord is G.

Upon further study of the C chord in harmony you will now notice the root (or C) is written in three part harmony. The 3rd (E) and 5th (G) are written in two part harmony.

Also, when you take a closer look at the F chord in harmony, you will now notice that the root (or F) is also written in three part harmony. The 3rd (A) and 5th (C) are written in two part harmony. The same with the G chord, the root (G) is written in three part harmony, the 3rd (B) and the 5th (D) are written in two part harmony.

A major chord can now be written three ways

1 - 3 - 5

or

Root, 3rd and 5th

or letters

C   E   G

THE CHORD SYMBOL ABOVE THE STAFF

The chord symbols over the staff will serve a two-fold purpose.

One: They will serve as a guide to the rhythm section as to which chord they are to play as accompaniment while the singer or instrumentalist performs the tune.

Two: They now serve as a guide telling you exactly what harmony notes you are to play. The harmony note normally being positioned <u>below</u> the melody note. The lead note is given in the above staff with the harmony for each note in parenthesis.

Remember your C, F and G harmony positions

measure # 1 .... The first two C notes (root) require three note harmony - the two F notes (root) all require three note harmony.

measure # 2 .... The first two G notes are two note harmony as they are the 5th of the C chord. The next two G notes require three note harmony as they are the root of G chord.

measure # 3 .... The first two note are played in two part harmony, being the 3rd of the F chord. The two "B" notes are also played in two part harmony as they are 3rd of the G chord.

measure # 4 .... The 1st C note (root) is played in three note harmony. The second note is played in two part harmony being the 5th of the F chord.

measure # 5 .... The "C" being the root of the chord is played in three part harmony.

ON TOP OF OLD SMOKEY

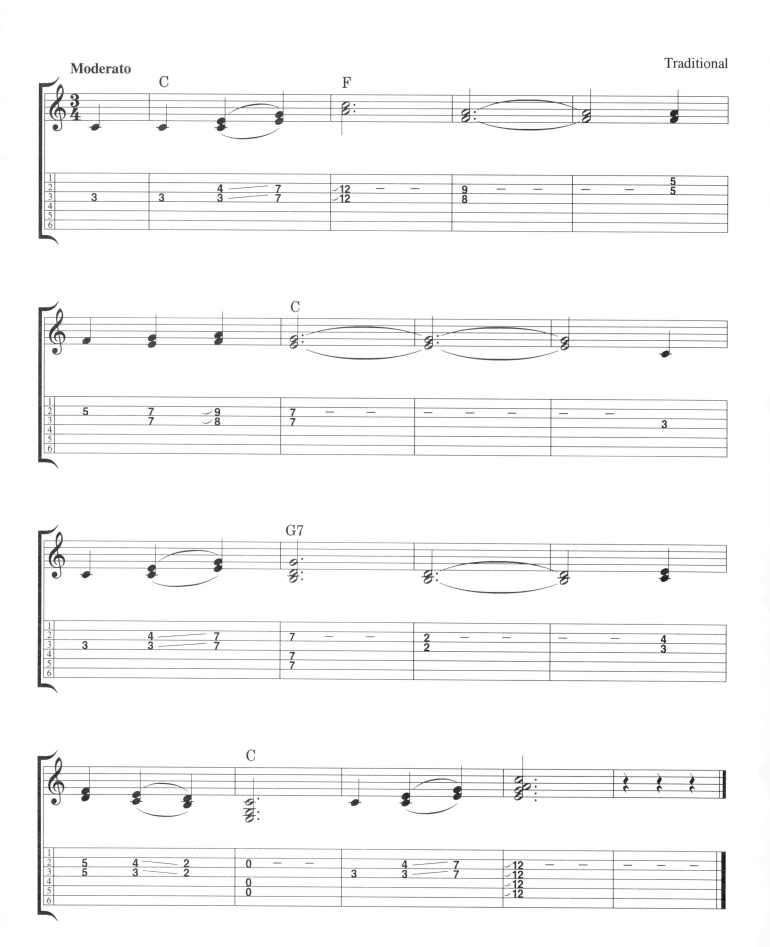

SWEET HOUR OF PRAYER

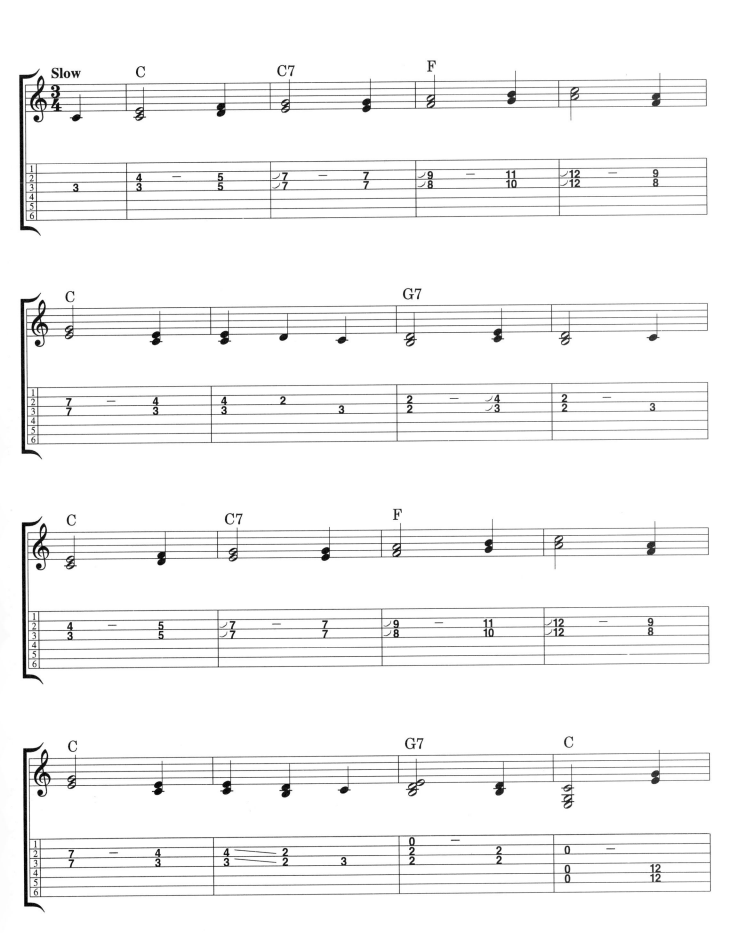

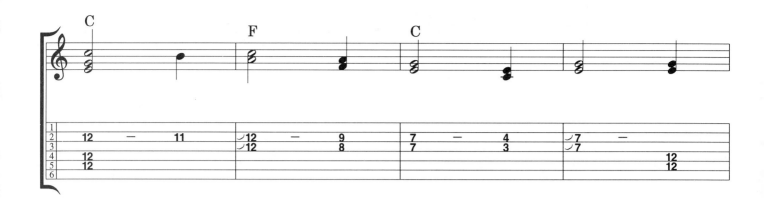

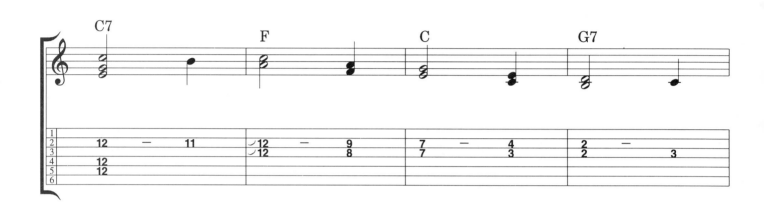

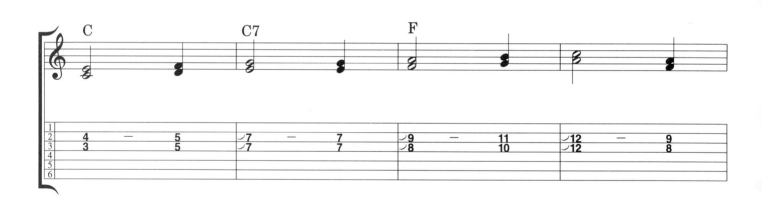

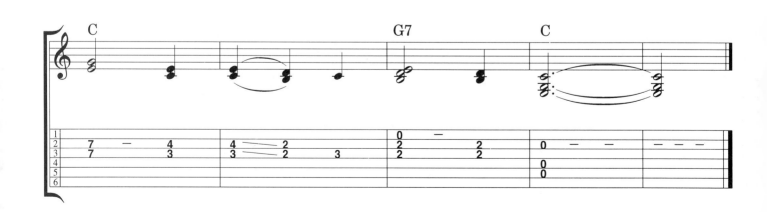

COUNTRY STYLE STEEL

by Dewitt Scott

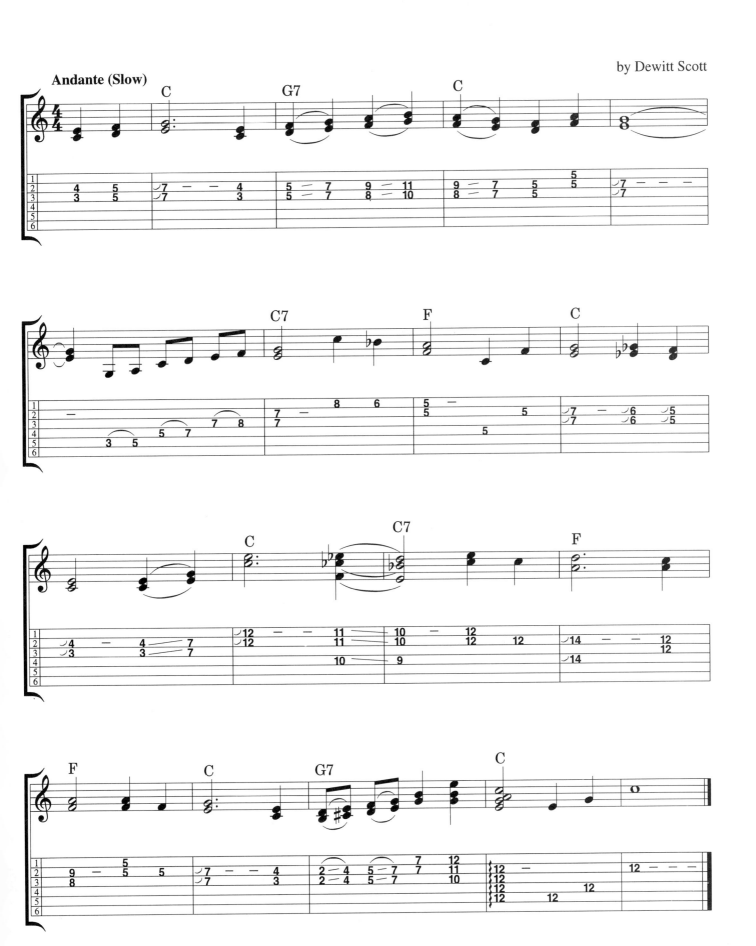

CAN I SLEEP IN YOUR BARN
TONIGHT MISTER?

Traditional

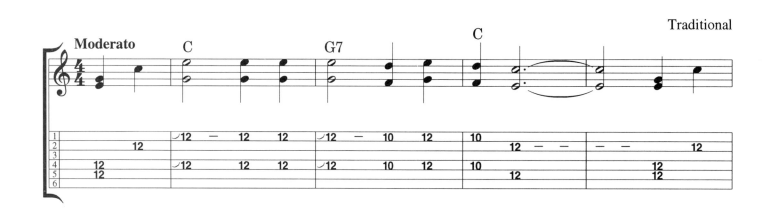

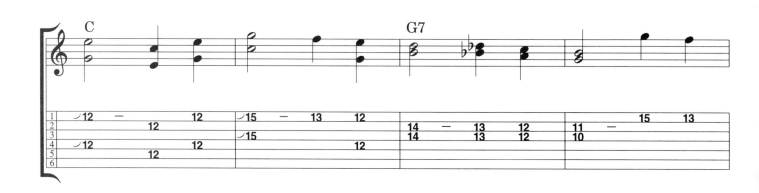

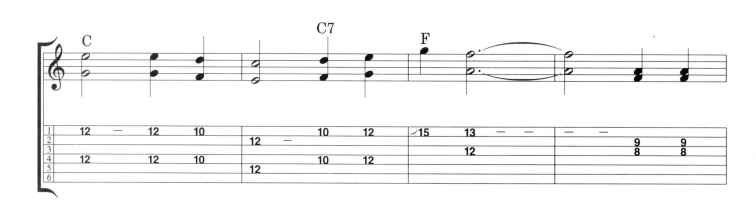

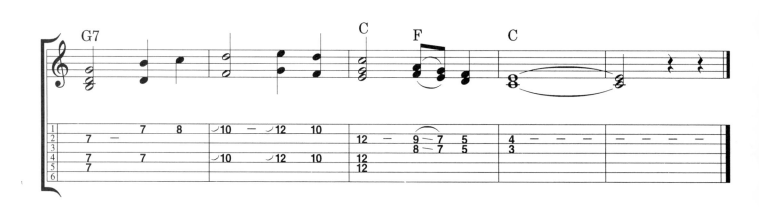

D.S. = Da Signa = Go back to the sign   Al Fine = The End

𝄋 = The Sign   Fine Pronounced = Feenay

Play the tune "The Scottish Waltz" completely thru - then go back to the 2nd line, 4th measure (𝄋) and

play to the G chord and the word Fine. The tune ends there.

THE SCOTTISH WALTZ

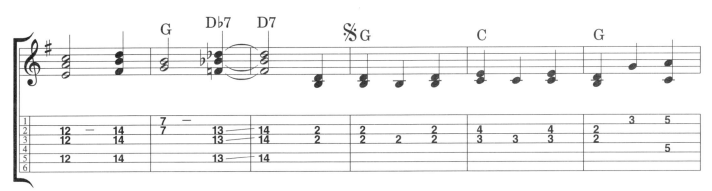

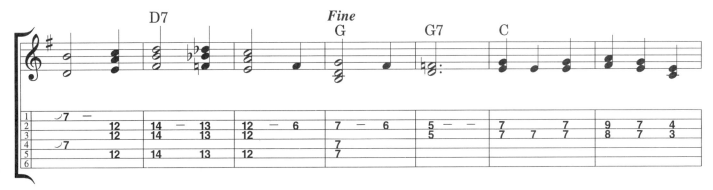

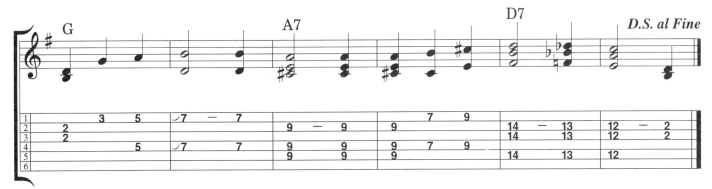

63

MINOR CHORDS

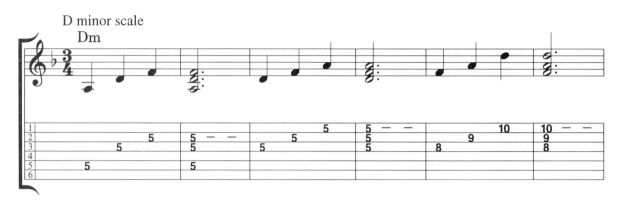

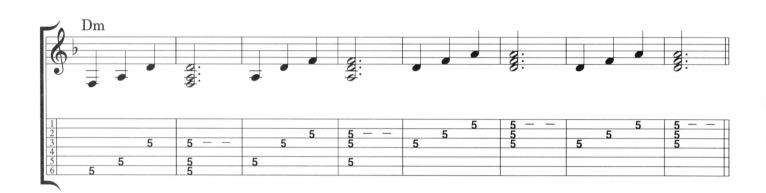

RULE FOR CONSTRUCTING THE MINOR CHORD

Root	Flatted 3rd	5th	*or*	1	3♭	5

Example

Major		Minor	
C Major Chord = C E G		C <u>minor</u> Chord = C E♭ G	
G Major Chord = G B D		G <u>minor</u> Chord = G B♭ D	
A Major Chord = A C♯ E		A <u>minor</u> Chord = A C E	
E Major Chord = E G♯ B		E <u>minor</u> Chord = E G B	

GREENSLEEVES

Old English Melody

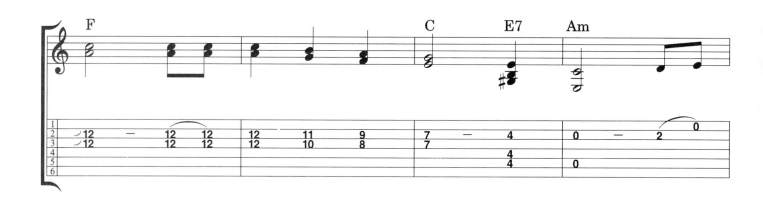

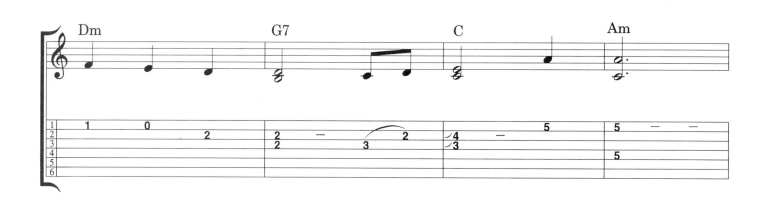

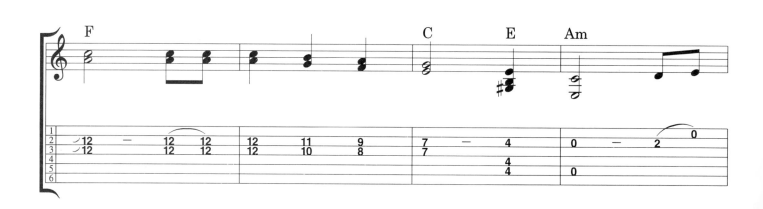

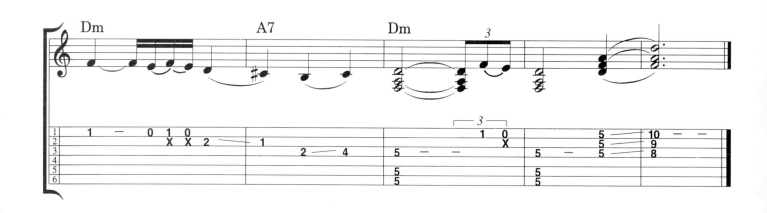

F SCALE AND CHORD POSITION

Key signature for F =      F Major Scale

When the flat sign is in the key signature all notes named B are played flat or one fret lower than normal.

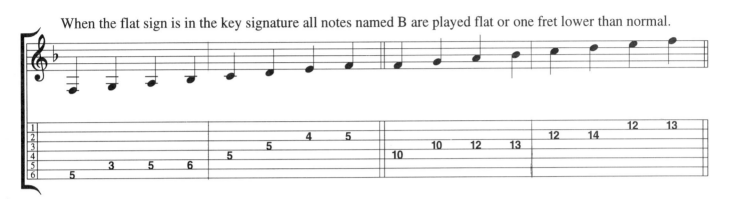

F SCALE HARMONIZED

THREE PRINCIPLE CHORD CHANGES IN F

F	Bb	C7
F A C	Bb D F	C E G Bb
(1)	(4)	(57th)

Their Positions

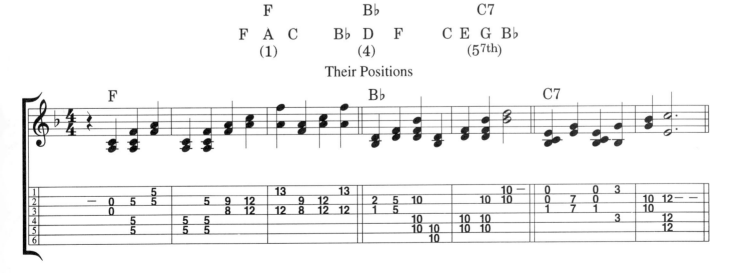

F SCALE IN THIRDS

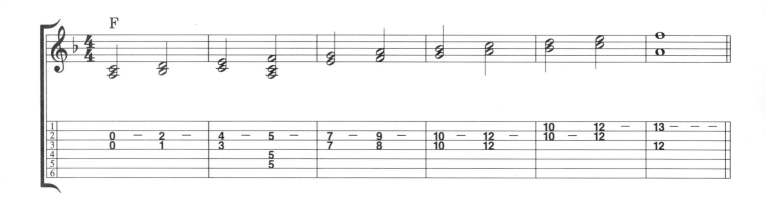

F SCALE IN SIXTH'S

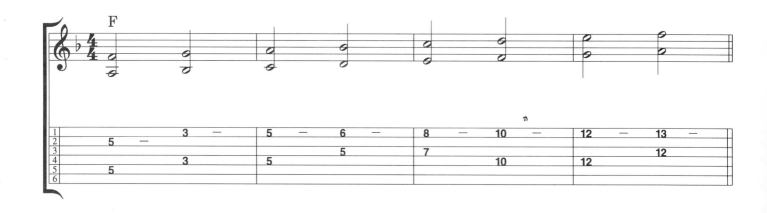

TRIPLET NOTE

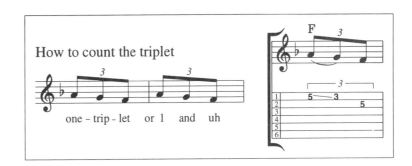

AMAZING GRACE

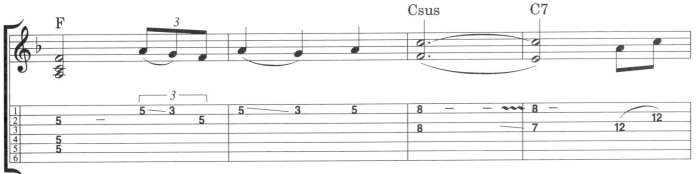

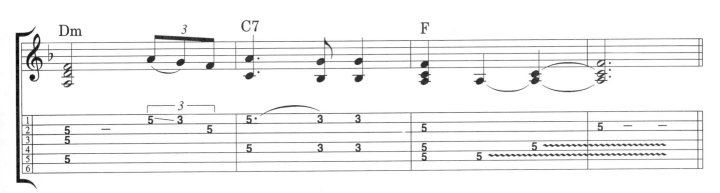

MY WILD IRISH ROSE

Traditional

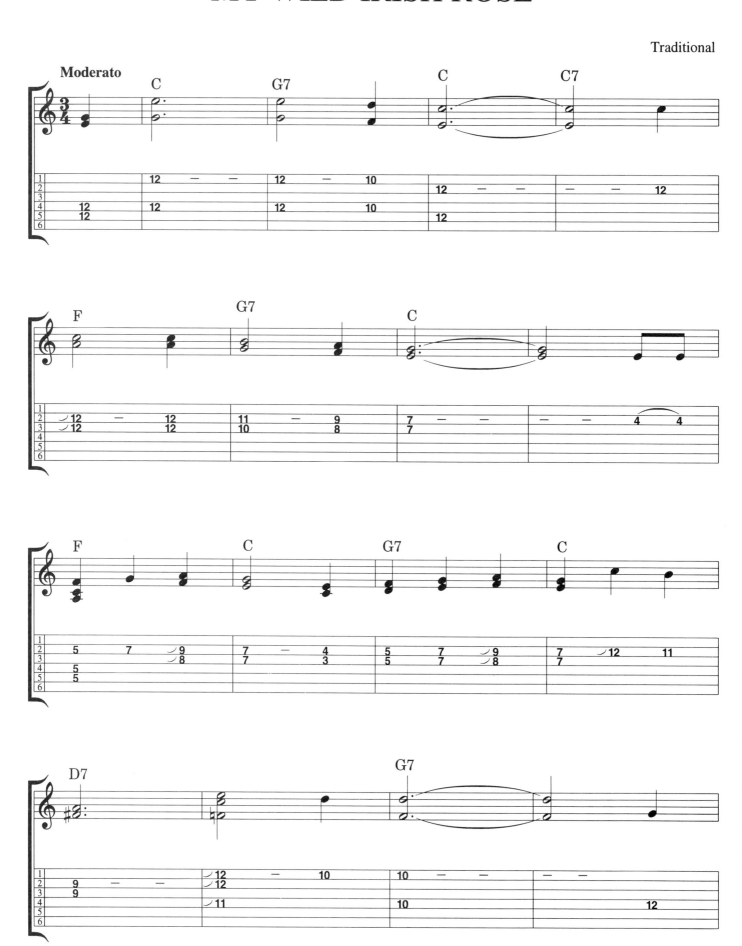

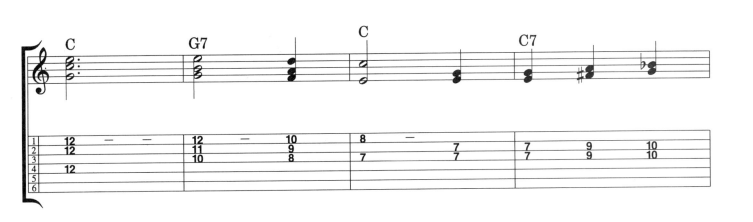

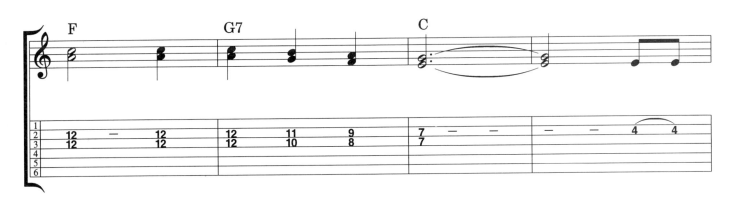

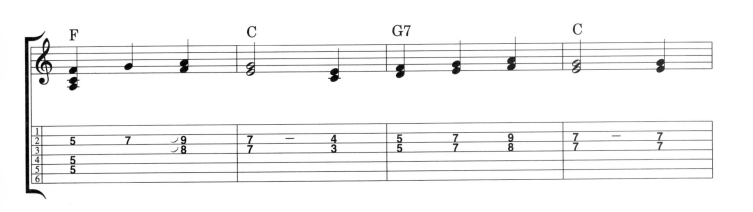

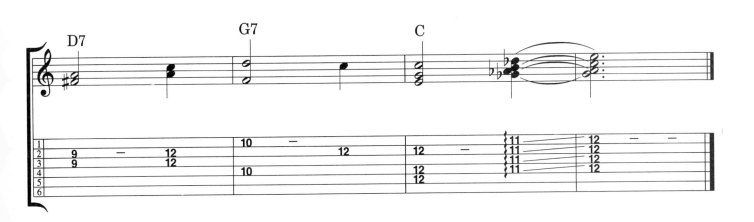

I'LL BE ALL SMILES TONIGHT

Traditional

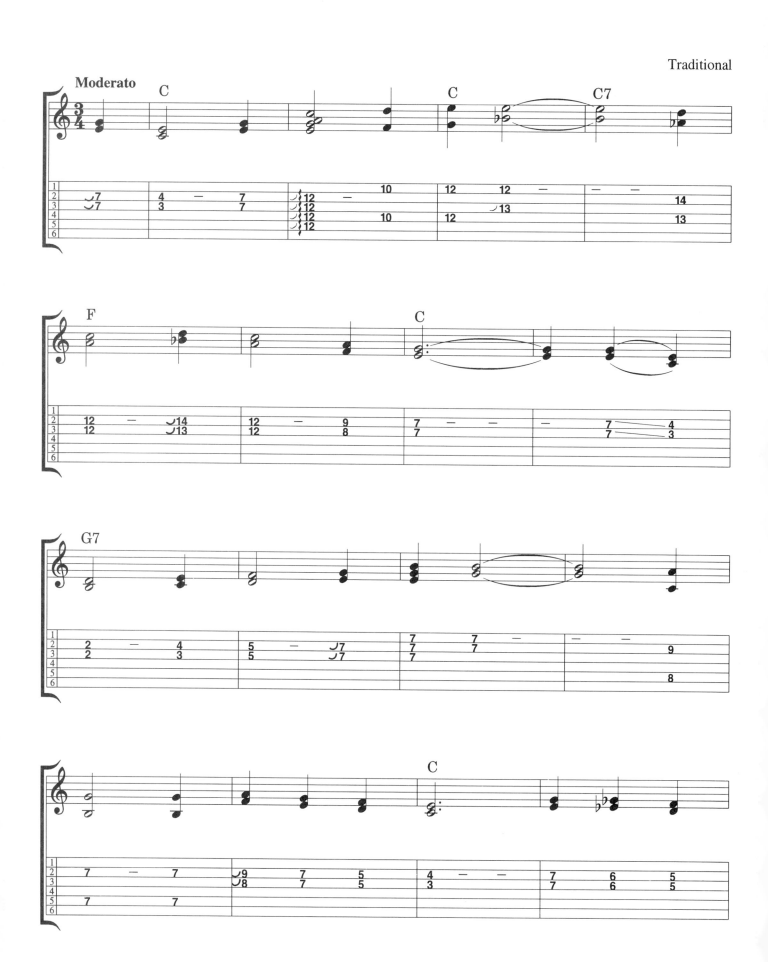

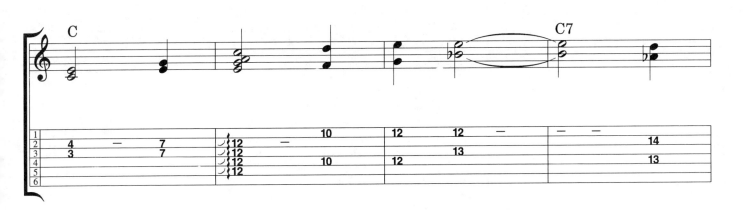

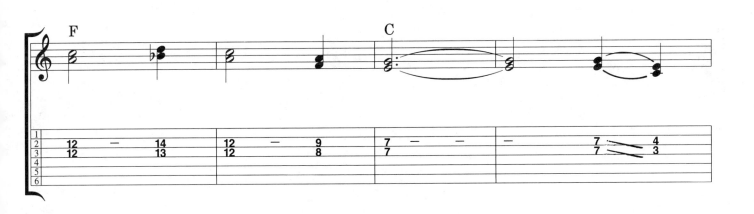

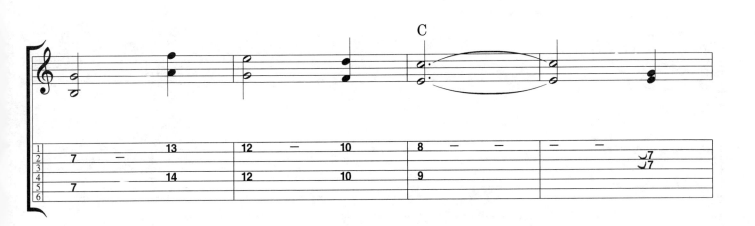

73

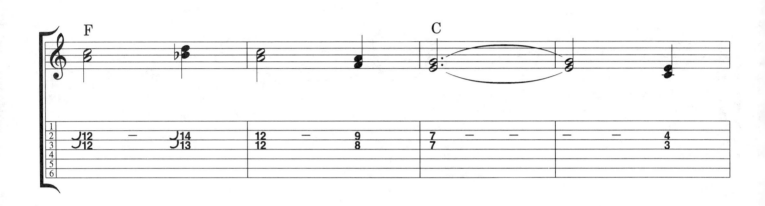

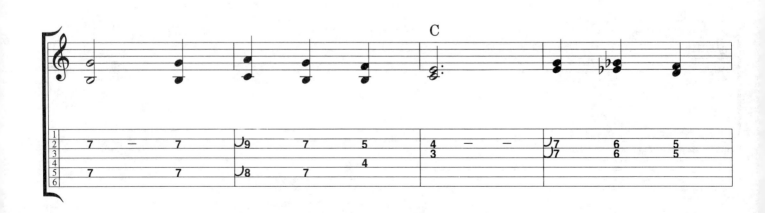

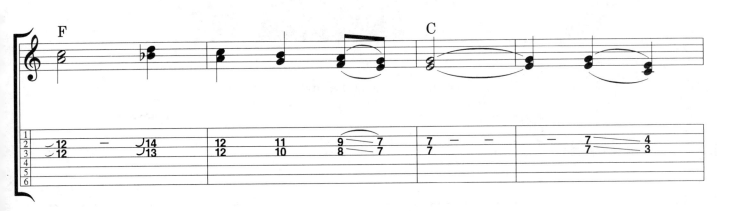

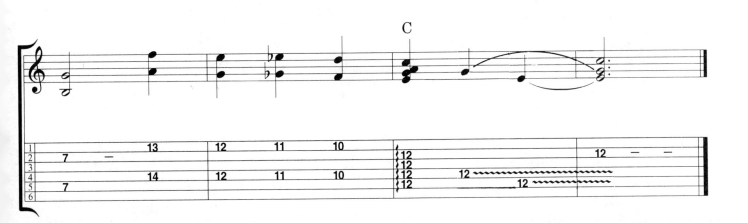

HARMONICS

This beautiful bell-like sound is executed with the left hand by placing the side of the little finger above the strings at the 12th fret. For an example, very lightly touch the second string with the little finger of the left hand at the 12th fret at the same time you pick it with the right hand. Treat the little finger like it touched a hot stove and raise it off the string immediately. The bell-like harmonic will then be sounded. The harmonic can also be played on the 5th, 7th, 19th and 24th frets as well as the 12th fret.

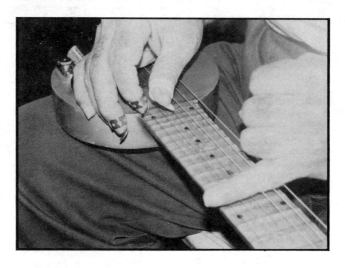

8va = Played an octave higher.

8va = An octave higher in pitch.
12va = An octave and a 5th higher in pitch.
16va = Two octaves higher in pitch.

Notice that the harmonics can be played easily at the 12th and 24th frets, fairly easy at the 7th and 19th frets, and a lot more difficult at the 5th fret. Complete tunes can be played with harmonics.

PALM HARMONICS

How to play harmonics when the bar is on any fret other than the open position with palm harmonics.

Palm harmonics are more difficult than the L.H. harmonics. They are executed by placing the side of the right hand (palm) 12 frets above the bar, resting lightly on the string to be picked. The "Hot Stove" rule applies here also. The thumb pick will be picking the string approximately four or five frets ahead of the palm. One odd fact about harmonics - the more you concentrate on them, the worse they sound. It has to be done "second nature" with some "guess work." You cannot see the fret the palm is on, so some judgement has to be used. Also, you must pick a little harder with the thumb, keeping the thumb close to the strings at all times.

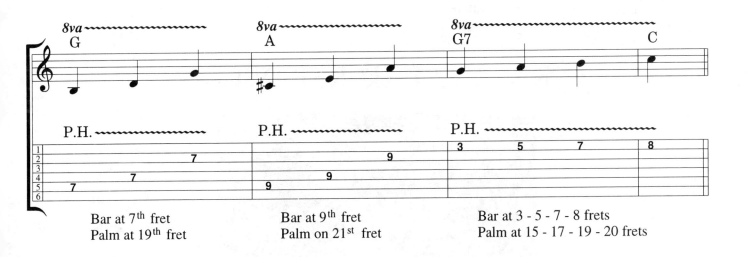

Bar at 7th fret
Palm at 19th fret

Bar at 9th fret
Palm on 21st fret

Bar at 3 - 5 - 7 - 8 frets
Palm at 15 - 17 - 19 - 20 frets

FINGER HARMONICS

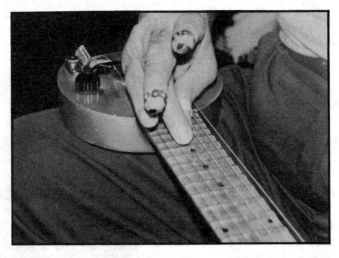

Another form of harmonics is the finger harmonic. You use the 3rd or ring finger of the right hand. You must place the center of the tip of the finger on the string on which you are to produce the harmonic. The thumb is tucked under the ring finger, actually anchored on the ring finger and stays there while the thumb picks the proper string. The thumb is now playing *behind* the finger instead of in front of it, as in the other harmonic positions. On a 15th fret harmonic the thumb will be picking the string at about the 18th fret.

KNUCKLE HARMONICS

This is the most difficult style but it is just as beautiful if not more clear than all the others. With this style, you tuck the 3rd and 4th fingers of the right hand under and lightly touch the string with the knuckle. It is a clear harmonic, especially when played close to the bar.

NOTE: With the knuckle and palm harmonic styles it is possible to pick one string with harmonics and another normally. This produces a very nice effect which we will demonstrate on the following pages.

ALOHA OE

Hawaiian Tune

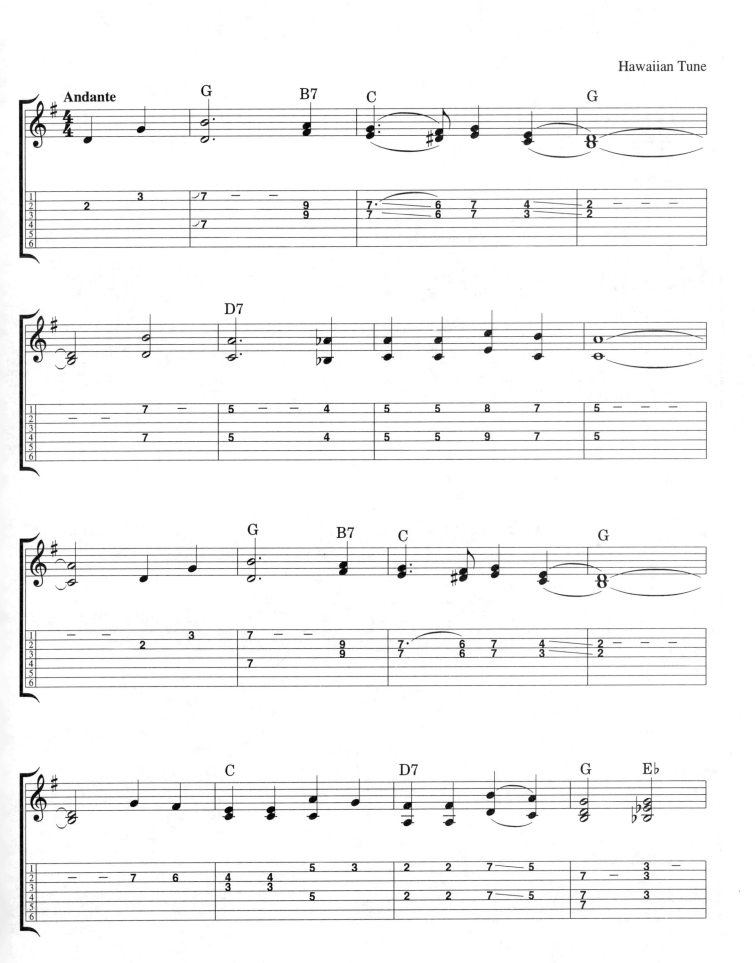

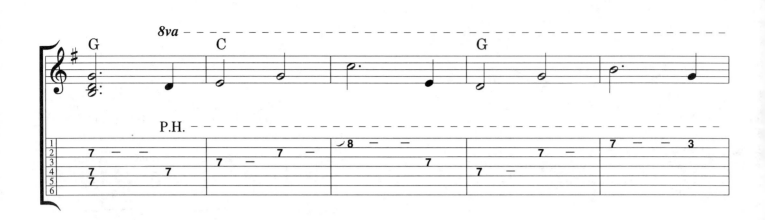

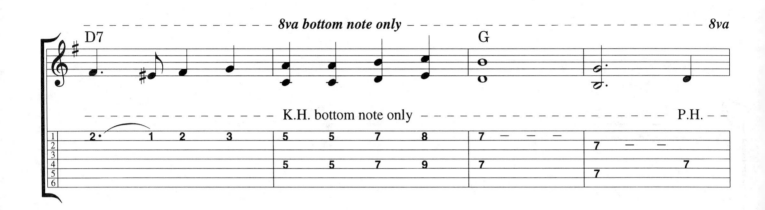

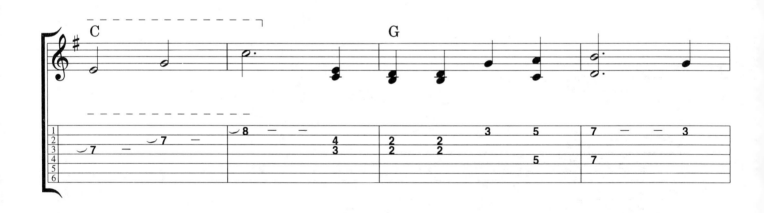

AURA LEE

Arranged by Herb Remington

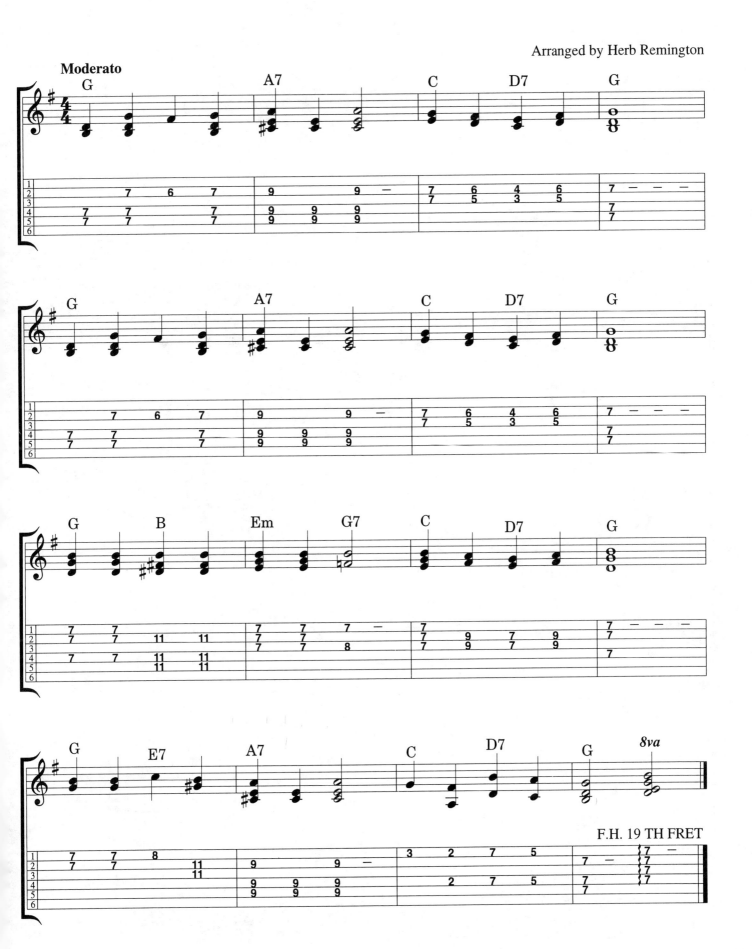

81

WABASH CANNONBALL

Traditional

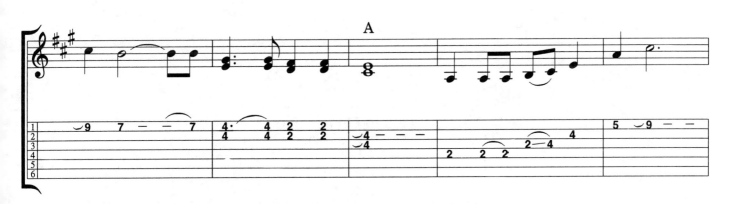

Counting Dual Measures

The top notes (stems up) have four counts.

The bottom notes (stems down) have four counts with the rest signs.

Triplets Tied to Quarter Note

SHENANDOAH

Traditional

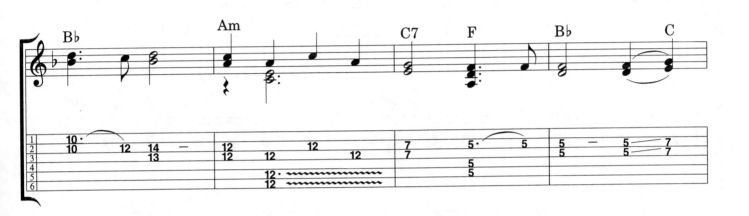

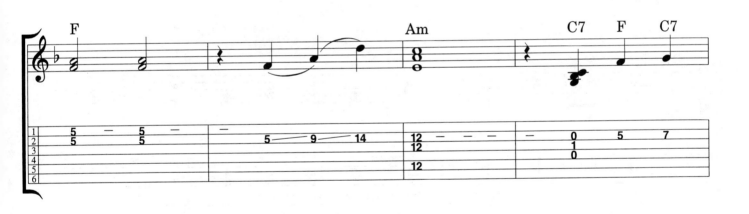

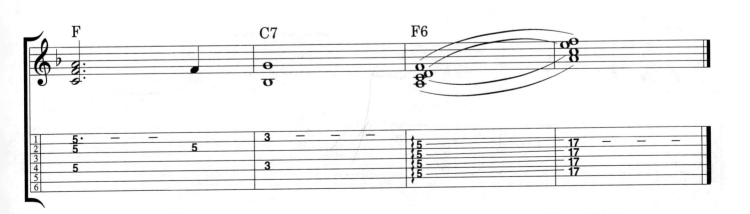

BYRDS

Dewitt Scott

THE GREAT SPECKLED BIRD

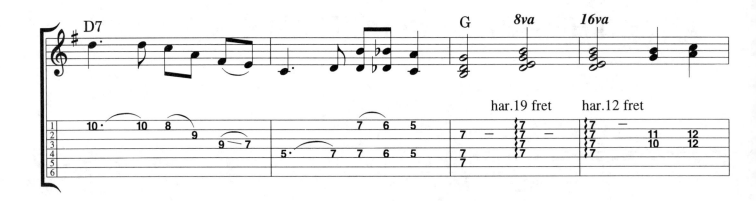

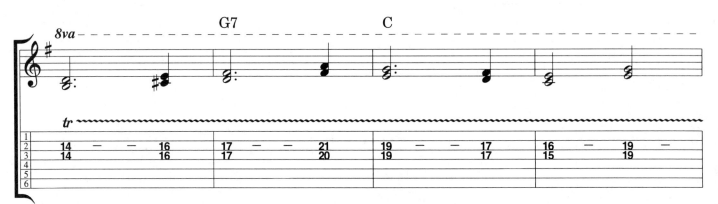

*tr – –*Trill. Rapidly alternating picking the two strings with the thumb and 1st finger. Starting with the thumb.

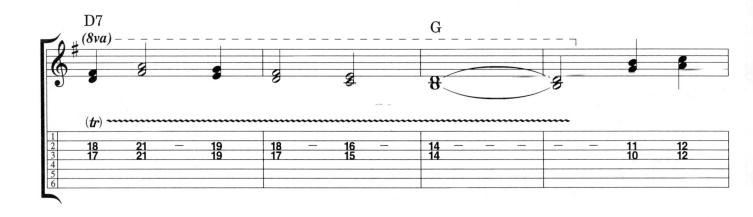

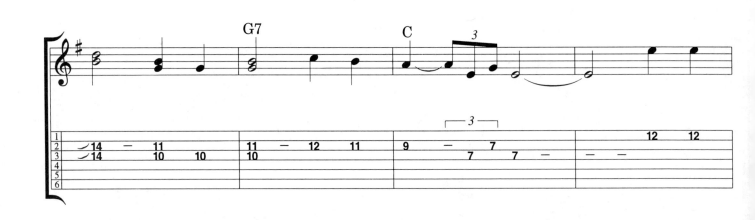

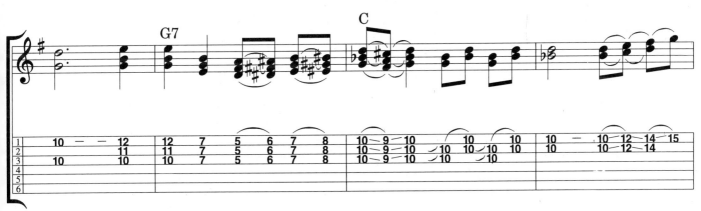

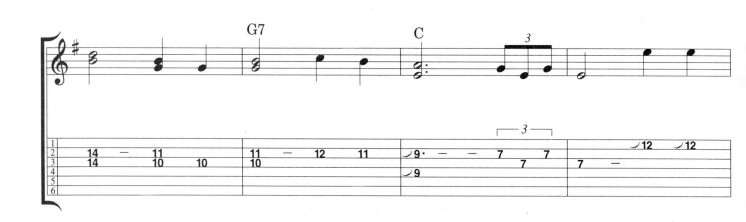

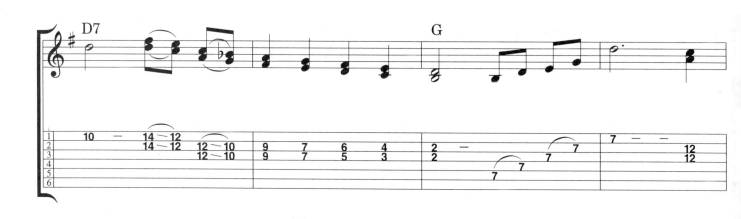

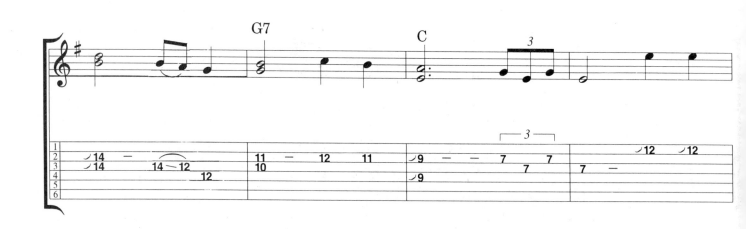

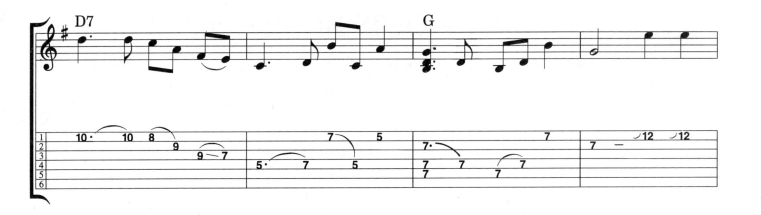

ST. LOUIS BLUES

Key of G

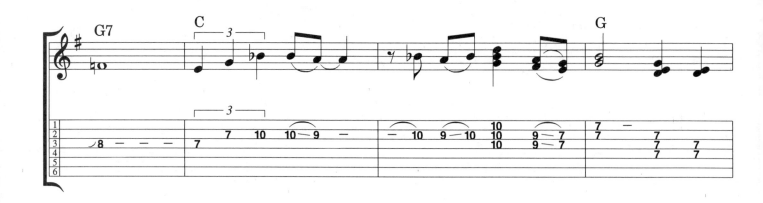

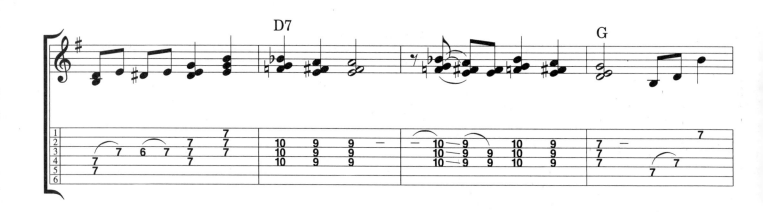

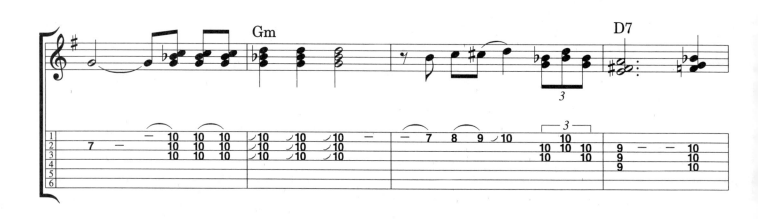

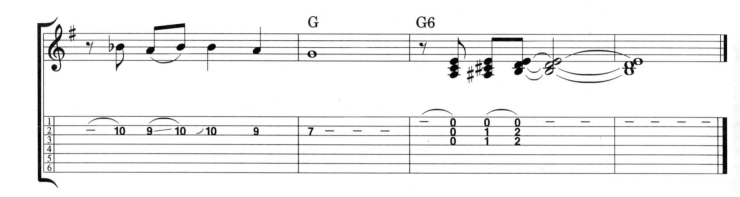

SLANT BAR AND "REVERSE" *SLANT* BAR INSTRUCTIONS

A *SLANT* BAR is required when one string is played on a certain fret and another string is played on another fret. As you are holding the bar, the thumb of the left hand is close to the end of the bar; to *slant* simply use the thumb to move the bar to the desired fret. To bring the bar back to its normal position, use the 3rd finger to help push the bar back. When you first *slant* the bar you actually move the entire hand forward, pushing the bar away from you yet staying on the desired frets. This is simply a finger movement- NOT an arm movement!

EXAMPLE:

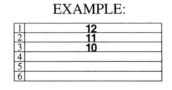

REVERSE *SLANT* BAR. Once again, move the bar to the desired fret with the thumb close to the end of the bar, pushing the entire hand away from you while staying on the desired frets. Pushing the bar away from you also applies when using a three-string *slant*. This is very important!

EXAMPLE:

EXAMPLE: